# AWAKE,
# ARISE,
# & ACT

# AWAKE, ARISE, & ACT

## A Womanist Call for Black Liberation

■ ■ ■

MARCIA Y. RIGGS

The Pilgrim Press
Cleveland, Ohio

The Pilgrim Press, Cleveland, Ohio 44115

© 1994 by Marcia Y. Riggs

Biblical quotations are from the New Revised Standard Version of the Bible,
© 1989 by the Division of Christian Education of the National Council of the
Churches of Christ in the U.S.A., and are used by permission

Printed in the United States of America on acid-free paper

99  98  97  96  95  94  5  4  3  2  1

Library of Congress Cataloging-in-Publication Data

Riggs, Marcia.

    Awake, arise, and act : a womanist call for Black liberation / Marcia Y.
Riggs.

      p.   cm.

    Includes bibliographical references and index.

    ISBN 0-8298-1009-9

    1. Afro-Americans—Social conditions—1975–  2. United States—Race
relations.  3. Afro-American women.  I. Title.

E185.86.R54   1994

305.896'073—dc20                      94-23378

                                               CIP

*To my mother and father,*
*Claudia Spurgeon Riggs and Sylvester Stephen Riggs, Jr.*

# Contents

# Preface

Lately, when I gather with black professionals at academic, church, or social functions, our conversations inevitably seem to turn to the ways the black community has become more and more divided—along class, gender, and political lines. We, members of the black middle class primarily by virtue of our education, professions, and income (in that order), speak often about the plight of our less advantaged brothers and sisters and our responsibility in the midst of growing antagonism, disunity, and death within the African American community. We bemoan the loss of black communal values and standards that were nurtured by our families (nuclear and extended, biological and "fictive kin"[1]) and to which we were held accountable in churches and schools of the segregated communities where we grew up. We ponder the wisdom and relevance of integration and its moral vision of the beloved community. To many of us, it seems that integration, at least in its present form, is morally bankrupt. Blacks today, and generations to come, will suffer from its damaging effects unless we can make a case for a new moral vision and more just social, political, and economic arrangements toward which we can strive.

I am a beneficiary of the work, culminating in integration, of people who gave their lives in civil rights movements, and I am deeply indebted and grateful to my courageous predecessors who envisioned and struggled for a better society. Their courage is my inspiration to envision a new struggle. I am of a transitional generation; we were not old enough to be leaders of the civil rights movement of the sixties, but our lives signify a transition in the black community from those who had the black community as their primary reference group to those who now struggle to reclaim our racial-cultural identity because integration has diminished our sense of community. Our task as a transitional generation must be to contribute a new phase to the civil rights movement: a black liberation movement. As an academically trained ethicist, my task is not discontinuous with the past but is part of a moral continuum involving fresh ethical reflection and moral agency for liberation.

These thoughts have been in my mind ever since I became aware, both personally and academically, of a relationship between white racism and divisiveness within the black community. I have had numerous encounters with black people that seemed inexplicable—until I began to understand that much of the anger and envy that we express toward one another derives from the internalization of destructive racist-sexist-classist social myths.

Through the writing of my own race-gender-class autobiography as part of teaching classes on the relationship between social processes and religion and how this relationship can perpetuate oppression, I have come to see the powerful social myths internalized by black people: universal equality, personal exceptionalism, and abstract injustice. These social myths have descriptive as well as prescriptive power in the individual and collective life of black people because each resonates with some religious, social, and/or political consciousness within the group. The social myth of universal equality derives from a belief that God created us as equals and that the U.S. constitution ensures that equality. The social myth of personal exceptionalism derives from the notion of individualism, which is at the heart of liberalism and the concept of private property. For blacks, it has meant striving to be, or be labeled as, an exceptional black person standing apart from the larger mass of poorer black people. The social myth of abstract injustice derives from the idea that we are captive to inextricable forces beyond our control, frequently referred to as "the system." This myth leads us into believing that there is no one from whom reparation and accountability for injustice can be claimed. For the religiously inclined, this myth is frequently interpreted as the inexplicable work of God's will; the faithful will get their just reward by and by. As is characteristic of any social myth, these contain an element of truth: there is equality in our creation, some black individuals are outstanding, injustice is systemic. However, mythic assumptions about social reality and our roles as members of racial, gender, and economic groups frequently obscure these truths. Thus we must find a way to be morally responsible in the face of social myths that distort, if not change, facts in order to undergird oppressive ways of life.[2]

By the conclusion of this book, I will have explored and suggested a way to be morally responsible in the midst of that social reality. I will propose a mediating ethic for black liberation with larger implications for the moral vision of the church into the twenty-first century. As a black Christian ethicist with a womanist agenda, I developed this ethic out of a particular methodology, presuppositions, and disciplinary perspectives outlined below.

The central theme of this study is liberation. To address this issue I will use an interdisciplinary approach to religious social ethics, with attention to history and social scientific theory.[3] Because liberation ethics require an explicit commitment to the struggle of particular groups of oppressed people, the use of what Beverly Harrison, a feminist Christian ethicist, terms a "sociohistorical ethical method" that engages the "stages of a liberation social ethics methodology"[4] further qualifies this approach. The seven stages of this methodology are:

1. *Establishing the entry point of conscientization* (clarifying the group's concrete historical experience of oppression or subjugation carried out communally)
2. *Explicit historical socioethical analysis* (aiming to connect historical narratives of specific, experienced oppression to the broader historical framework)
3. *Careful examination of the roots and ongoing dynamics of oppression or subjugation* (recognizing that the past is embedded in present social relations)
4. *Clarification of solidarities and loyalties* (solidarity with the marginalized and oppressed)
5. *Clarification of a movement's options for action*
6. *Examination of strategic options in light of the moral norms espoused in and intrinsic to the liberation process itself*

7. *Application of the hermeneutic of liberation to the internal history of Christianity itself* (scrutinizing and reengaging Scripture and tradition through critical awareness of the existing situation)[5]

My interpretation of religious social ethics adapts the method and stages of liberation social ethics methodology.

# Acknowledgments

I am grateful to God, and I thank family, friends, and colleagues who have supported my efforts to bring this book to fruition. To my family, thanks for being understanding even when you did not understand why I felt compelled to write this book. To my friends, thanks for listening to my joys and my tears as I struggled. To my colleagues, thanks for inviting me into your institutional settings where I was able to test some of my ideas with a larger audience.

My special thanks to: the members of my dissertation committee at Vanderbilt University because much of that dissertation is present in this work: Howard Harrod, Peter Paris, Peter Hodgson, Lewis V. Baldwin, and Karen Campbell; members of the Womanist Approaches to Religion and Society Group of the American Academy of Religion, particularly Emilie Townes, Katie Cannon, Delores S. Williams, Cheryl Townsend Gilkes; the Fund for Theological Education without whose financial support I would not have made it; student assistants, Christine Isham Walsh, Tim Simpson, and Sherri Simpson; Thomas Ogletree, who was the dean who empowered this young scholar during my first full-time teaching appointment at Drew Theological School to develop my scholarship; Peter Paris, who taught me much about the discipline of ethics and who continues to be a moral exemplar as mentor and friend; Richard Brown at Pilgrim Press for giving me my first chance to become a published author; and Mary Ann Bowers, Joan Speaks, and Ellen Armour, who have been friends above and beyond the call of duty.

# Introduction

This book analyzes the moral dilemma that social stratification in the black community poses for black liberation and the ethical praxis needed to address that dilemma. I trace the development of competitive individualism versus intragroup social responsibility in the black community—a dilemma at the center of social stratification and black oppression today. I employ historical and contemporary voices from the black community to aid me in describing and analyzing the dilemma as well as in proposing a praxis (theory and action) for black liberation. In particular, I turn to reformers in the black women's club movement from the late nineteenth and early twentieth centuries to explicate a socioreligious ethical perspective on this dilemma. My contention is that the club movement offers a distinctive perspective and paradigm that is an important resource for black liberation ethical reflection. Three suppositions undergird this contention.

First, the need for this analysis arises from my membership in the black community and my commitment to the struggle of black people in the United States to effect liberation from the continuing consequences of historically generated racial oppression. Accordingly, my understanding of a womanist[1] agenda and perspective as well as the tasks of a black womanist religious scholar determines my worldview:

1. The black women's experience is inextricably bound with the struggle of black people for liberation from race, gender, and class oppression in the United States.
2. The womanist perspective has as a fundamental guiding premise a principle of collective solidarity. This means that

black women understand their individual autonomy to be in-
terdependent with the collective position of Blacks in this
country.
3. Womanists engage in at least four tasks: (a) uncovering the
roots of a womanist tradition through examination and reinte-
gration of black women's experience into black history in particular and American history in general; (b) debunking social
myths so as to undermine the black woman's acceptance of
sexist oppression, the black man's acceptance of patriarchal
privilege, and the white woman's acceptance of white racist
privilege; (c) constructing black womanist theology and religious ethics in light of the first two tasks and to broaden these
disciplines to include nontraditional bases and sources for
theological and ethical reflection; (d) envisioning *human liberation* (not solely racial/ethnic-group or gender-group liberation) under God; that is, black womanists are proposing a
*decidedly inclusive* perspective that is acutely aware of the need
for the simultaneous liberation from all oppression.

Second, there are two interrelated, yet distinguishable, issues
that must be considered in order to grasp the complexity of black
oppression: (1) The *intergroup dynamics* between Blacks as an oppressed group and the white racist, patriarchal, capitalist U.S. society, because these dynamics comprise *an external dimension of
black oppression*; and (2) the *intragroup dynamics* among Blacks as
an oppressed group whose life situation is rooted in a common
history of struggle against racist-patriarchal-capitalist oppression
in the U.S., because these express *an internal dimension of black
oppression*. The focus on social stratification within the black
community signifies the need to reflect ethically upon black oppression from the perspective of Blacks ourselves. The ethical
analysis of intragroup dynamics among black people is primary,
I contend, for effecting liberation in this society, because intragroup dynamics either foster or undermine the communal
consciousness that is a precondition for black liberation.

Third, the tasks of a liberation ethicist are descriptive, critical,
and normative.[2] In this analysis, the descriptive task is to describe
the roots of competitive individualism versus intragroup social
responsibility as derived from social stratification within the
black community. Awareness of the roots of this dilemma is nec-

essary for understanding the ongoing dynamics of the internal dimension of black oppression. The critical task is to assess the responses of Blacks themselves to the ethical dilemma as embodied in their race-class and race-gender-class consciousness and ideologies for racial advancement in the United States. The normative task is to appropriate critically the historical responses in an attempt to establish the groundwork for a mediating ethic for black liberation.

From the presuppositions of a womanist agenda and acceptance that there are external and internal dimensions of black oppression, it is evident that black oppression is more complex than simply race oppression—particularly from the perspective of black women's experience and history. As Manning Marable suggests,

> *From the dawn of the slave trade until today, U.S. capitalism was both racist and deeply sexist. The superexploitation of Black women became an important feature in American social and economic life, because sisters were assaulted simultaneously as workers, as Blacks, and as women. . . . To understand the history of all Blacks within the Black majority, the 'domestic Black periphery,' special emphasis is required in documenting the particular struggles, ideals, and attitudes of Black women. . . . Black male liberationists must relearn their own history, by grounding themselves in the wisdom of their sisters.*[3]

A sociohistorical ethical method for liberation ethics requires that it be experientially grounded; black women's experience and history is that ground. It provides the model for analyzing the complexity of black oppression because black women, through their existence, face the tri-dimensional phenomenon of race-gender-class oppression. Also, there are specific trends in black and women's historiography that offer theoretical avenues for using black women's experience and history as an appropriate starting point for this ethical reflection.

One trend in black historiography is a periodization (i.e., slavery, emancipation, urbanization) that recognizes the centrality of "how the social labor of blacks was mobilized and reproduced" and the use of class as an interpretative construct.[4]   Concurrent with this trend is research addressing the culture and solidarity of the black community from the perspective of the masses, which has begun to uncover class divisions and tensions between black masses and black elites.[5] Black historical research on emancipation and urbanization is now developing important lines of investigation into these areas: the type of social differentiation among the newly freed, the pursuit of autonomy through community and institution building, the relationship between urbanization and social class differentiation, and the significance of black women's participation through their clubs and as individuals to the development of black communities throughout the various periods of black history.[6] Thus, the analysis of social stratification and the use of black women's experience and history align with these concerns of black historiography.

Likewise, the trend in women's historiography to recognize women as distinct sociohistorical groups leads to documenting and reinterpreting history from the perspective of women as social agents: "The most interesting and significant aspect of the history of women as a field is its potential for showing us that females, handicapped or not, did things as individuals and groups that affected the structure, functioning and historical unfolding of their societies."[7]

Further, the recognition of women as distinct sociohistorical groups has led to acknowledgment of distinctions within the shared experience of women and men as well as diversity among women. For instance, middle-class women and men did (and do) not live comparable lives because of constraints on women's lives,[8] nor were (or are) the lives of middle-class black women analogous to the lives of middle-class white women.[9] The use of black women's experience and history to focus this analysis means acknowledging the distinct social agency of black women with respect to both black men and white women; in brief, documenting black history from the black women's perspective. In this case, this means recognizing black women as social reformers in their own right and adding their work and insights to the base of knowledge for ethical reflection regarding black liberation.

More specifically, the importance of black women's experience and history to this analysis derives from "the dialectics of black womanhood,"[10] here referring to the fact that the experience and history of black women originated and evolves in a distinct reality wherein the forces of race-gender-class oppression converge. During the nineteenth century, black women confronted the tensions of their distinct reality by affirming dialectically their race-gender-class identity through a sense of obligation and duty to Blacks as a group. Understanding this sense of obligation and duty is important for discerning the kind of intragroup social responsibility needed to address the present oppression of Blacks.

The quest for a mediating ethic for black liberation with intragroup social responsibility as its core value is an attempt to formulate an ethic of responsibility for the black community. The hermeneutic of liberation thus requires dialogical and critical engagement with the theme of responsibility that can be found in traditional religious ethics.

Generally, there are two principles underlying the theme of responsibility in ethics: accountability and commitment. In religious ethics, this means that responsibility is "intended to convey both the total inescapable relation of [the person] to the judgment and grace of his[/her] Creator and Redeemer as well as his[/her] involvement in the discrete activities required of the moral [person]." In effect, there is "an intertwining of theological and ethical accountability," and responsibility is used by religious ethicists to address "a problem of unification: the problem of the relation between a transcendent God and human morality."[11]

More specifically, in applying the hermeneutic of liberation, I will bring the understanding of responsibility as represented by H. Richard Niebuhr's ethic of responsibility into critical engagement with the ethical insights of black women reformers. The aim of this dialogue is twofold. First, it is my intent as a black Christian liberation ethicist who affirms a womanist agenda to try to "balance the paradigms and assumptions of this intellectual tradition [regarding responsibility] with a new set of questions arising from the context of Black women's lives."[12] Thus it is important to examine how the black women reformers' understanding of responsibility agrees with and/or extends the meaning of responsibility in Niebuhr's ethic and serves as the basis of a mediating ethic for black liberation. Second, it is important to discern the further implications of the club women's ethical perspective for a mediating ethic that addresses the church.

The outline of the book is as follows. In Chapter 1, I identify key sociological perspectives, terms, and constructs for understanding the quest for black liberation. Chapter 2 is a discussion of the sociological debate about the impact of race and class on black life today and a reinterpretation of that debate. In Chapter 3, I describe the origin and evolution of social stratification to uncover the roots of the present dilemma in the black community. This narrative uses sociological and historical sources to interpret black life during the late nineteenth century into the early twentieth century. In Chapter 4, I present the response of black women to the dilemma in terms of their race-gender-class consciousness and the thought and work of the black women's club movement. In Chapter 5, the perspective of the club women is brought into dialogue with H. Richard Niebuhr's ethic of responsibility, black liberation, and womanist religious thought, with special attention to ethical praxis to overcome black oppression. I also assess the way in which the club women's response is paradigmatic for responding to the dilemma today. In Chapter 6, I discuss the relevance of the club movement's ethical perspective for rethinking moral vision, moral agency, and Christian ethical reflection in the larger church community. The final chapter, Chapter 7, is a sermonic fragment that illustrates a mediating process of Christian ethical reflection.

# I

# A Sociology of Black Liberation

In this book, sociology is understood as "critical humanism." Sociology as critical humanism seeks to account for the observable behavior of people as well as the meaning people assign to their behavior. It also analyzes destructive forces in society and examines trends that might counter such forces.[1]

More specifically, I am informed by black sociology that challenges studies premised upon so-called objectivity because these studies, in fact, perpetuate racist values.[2] In fact, this study affirms the ideological intent of black social science, which "combines an interpretation of the social world with a moral commitment to change it."[3]

That combination of social analysis and moral commitment thus undergirds a sociology of black liberation. The task of a sociology of black liberation is "to study Black American life and culture as an internal social system while understanding the external constraints on Black lives and institutions"[4] and to "subject to social analysis and criticism those Black institutions and behavioral patterns that not only do not meet the needs of Black people but serve as an impediment to unifying the Black community."[5]

Informing this discussion are the following presuppositions derived from the understanding of sociology as a critical humanism and a sociology of black liberation: social stratification within U.S. society is a destructive force in need of analysis so as to uncover countertrends that promote fullness of life for Blacks and all U.S. citizens;[6] quantitative and interpretative analyses of social stratification in U.S. society, generally and within the black community particularly, provide the "data" for this analysis; and social stratification within the black community is subjected to critical analysis as a behavioral pattern that impedes black liberation.

## Social Stratification and the Structure
## of Social Inequality in the United States

Beth Vanfossen suggests that social stratification is "structured social inequality" consisting of institutionalized power arrangements that "perpetuate intergenerational patterns of economic, political, and prestige inequalities." Closely aligned is a class system that is present when noticeable boundaries exist in terms of "interactive patterns, exclusivity, and degree of self-consciousness." The boundaries of such a system, according to Vanfossen, are not as distinct and rigid as those found in a caste system. Vanfossen also points out two types of class consciousness: *corporate* class consciousness, in which individuals "believe that their own life chances depend on the actions and success of the class as a whole with which they identify," and *competitive* class consciousness, in which "individuals believe that their life chances depend on their own personal effort and resources in competition with other individuals in the society."[7] Vanfossen's definition of the structure of social inequality, multidimensionality of social stratification, and distinction between types of class consciousness thus inform this analysis.

Popular belief holds that the United States has an open-class system whereby individuals can achieve upward social mobility through ambition and hard work. From a conflict perspective, however, which exposes domination and exploitation as primary features of a class system, this is not the case. A "conflict model with systemic assumptions"[8] describes a structure of social inequality operative through the "capitalist democracy"[9] of the United States that is legitimated by an ideology of egalitarianism, which is maintained through the legal, educational, religious, and familial institutions. In contrast to the ideology of egalitarianism, actual social mobility in U.S. society is highly correlated with an individual's original family class position as well as his or her race and gender.[10]

Blacks or other ethnics of color find that their chances for social mobility are further restrained by "a second and equally power-ful system [of] ethnic stratification,"[11] which assigns groups designated places in society on the basis of a social distance scale, which in turn is based upon white Eurocentric norms and standards of social acceptability. This system has two significant ramifications. On the one hand, Blacks and other ethnics of color (primarily because of their color) experience restricted social mobility and are found disproportionately in the lower positions in the class system. On the other hand, there is a tendency for Blacks and other ethnics of color to develop their own systems of stratification, which, as James Blackwell has suggested, is "superimposed on and overlaid by the larger one."[12]

My analysis, then, proceeds from this assumption: that the structures of social inequality and ethnic stratification provide the context within which the social stratification of the black community occurs. This assumption is crucial if this analysis is not to degenerate into a diatribe of "blaming the victim."[13] For it is possible that an analysis of social stratification of the black community could be construed as asserting that the black community is trapped by class divisions that reflect a desire by Blacks as individuals for social mobility that allows them to assimilate into American society, and this has created a divisiveness that is the *sole* reason why Blacks as a group cannot attain black liberation. Thus Blacks are held solely responsible for the limited successes of efforts for black liberation. However, this analysis contends that the structure of social inequality operative in the society is the *constitutive* factor in the oppression of Blacks—an external dimension—whereas social stratification within the black community is a *derivative* factor—an internal dimension—that impedes black liberation.

## Black Community and Social Stratification

What do I mean by the term "black community"? From a sociological perspective, there are two general definitions of community: a "territorial" or "ecological" usage and a "relational" or "sociopsychological" one.[14] Although case studies of particular territorial (geographical) black communities will provide significant empirical evidence for this analysis, the primary meaning of black community in this discussion is relational or sociopsychological. This definition holds that Blacks as a group in the United States share a common identity and have "special claims on each other."[15] This communal identity originates in a common history of oppression in the conflict with white Euroamericans, one grounded in both past enslavement and continuing discrimination.[16]

Thus, "black community" signifies a group whose communal identity is rooted in a common history of survival.[17] Yet I will suggest that despite this common history, social stratification has weakened black communal consciousness—i.e., the relational sense of Blacks having special claims on one another—and has thus impeded efforts toward black liberation.

Given that social stratification within the black community is a derivative factor of black oppression, what theoretical framework is useful for a descriptive analysis of stratification within the black community? The concepts of parallel structures, internal colonialism, and systems theory[18] as well as a paradigm for the study of class consciousness create that framework.

When the concept of parallel structures is applied to the black community, social stratification within the community represents a condition of black life that parallels life in society overall. This means that although social stratification exists in society generally, social stratification within the black community may exhibit both structural and valuational differences from the larger society.[19]

Second, the perspective of internal colonialism asserts that "in many respects the [black] community exists only in a colonized state, since much of what occurs in it is controlled and manipulated by a power structure that is external to the community itself. The manipulation from the outside is only partial, however, since a structure prevails within the community itself."[20] Social stratification within the black community should thus be assessed in terms of the subordinate racial group status of black Americans historically and presently and the possible existence and role of a colonized black elite.[21] Further, this perspective views class divisions in the black community as a tactic of capitalist exploitation, creating distinctions that produce conflict and weaken solidarity for resistance against oppression.[22]

Third, when the black community is construed as a social system, it is perceived that "a significant segment [of the community] share norms, sentiments and expectations. . . . Even though diversity exists within the community, its members are held together by adherence to commonly shared goals."[23] Social stratification within the black community is thus evaluated in terms of how increasing class consciousness undermines a corporate race consciousness of commonly shared goals.

Accordingly, a paradigm for the study of class consciousness that focuses upon class consciousness as "a *processual* emergent" that should be studied in a dynamic framework, either historical or biographical,[24] can be utilized to understand social stratification in the black community. This paradigm defines class consciousness as based upon economic criteria and encourages comparison of other aspects of stratum consciousness, such as race and gender.[25] A comparison of class-race-gender consciousnesses from a "contextual interactive perspective"[26] advances a description of the race-class consciousness of Blacks generally in relation to the race-gender-class consciousness of black women. This paradigm also allows the examination of objective (e.g., occupation, income, influence, or power) and subjective (e.g., ideologies, attitudes, aspirations) criteria of stratification to explain the relationship of Blacks to one another and to society overall.

In sum, this descriptive analysis of social stratification within the black community presupposes that class consciousness develops historically and that differing kinds of class consciousness are comparative and interactive. In other words, the dilemma of competitive individualism versus intragroup social responsibility has its basis in both socioeconomic realities and a race-class consciousness that has evolved throughout black history. The race-gender-class consciousness of black women offers an alternative perspective for analyzing this dilemma.

## Black Liberation

Black liberation may be described as the desire of black citizens to achieve more than integration into U.S. society. That is, whereas integration seeks the inclusion of Blacks in terms of reform within U.S. society, black liberation seeks the inclusion of Blacks in terms of radical change in society itself. To reiterate: the aim of black liberation is to transform the structure of U.S. society, recognizing structural barriers grounded in institutional racism and capitalist exploitation. To desire black liberation is to recognize and confront an assertion such as this:

> *Blacks occupy the lowest socioeconomic rung in the ladder of American upward mobility precisely because they have been 'integrated' all too well into the system. America's 'democratic' government and 'free enterprise' system are structured deliberately and specifically to maximize Black oppression. Capitalist development has occurred not in spite of the exclusion of Blacks, but because of the brutal exploitation of Blacks as workers and consumers. Blacks have never been equal partners in the American Social Contract, because the system exists not to develop but to* underdevelop *Black people.*[27]

Moreover, the goal of black liberation requires that black people recognize their continuing *subordinate group status* within American society. Black liberation requires *group* rather than *individual* progress. Insofar as the aim of black liberation is collective advancement, the goal has affinities with black nationalism, which has as its objective the cultural, economic, social, and political self-determination of black people. As James Turner has written, "There develops the firm conviction that Afro-Americans must become transmuted into a conscious and cohesive group. The rationale is that a group giving a unitary response can more effectively and honorably confront the constraining dominant group. . . . Loyalty to group cultural attributes and commitment to collective goals provide the adhesive for the group."[28]

Black liberation, therefore, refers to collective advancement for Blacks with the goal of transforming the economic and political structure of American society. The goal is ideologically nationalistic in that it emphasizes the need for black people to engender and sustain a communal identity. Black communal consciousness is critical to an ethic for black liberation. The contention here is that the social stratification of Blacks is a factor that undermines black communal consciousness and, consequently, black liberation.

# 2
# The Race versus Class Debate: A Socioethical Dilemma

Debate as to whether race or class is more determinative of black life chances in the United States today was initiated primarily by William J. Wilson in *The Declining Significance of Race: Blacks and Changing American Institutions.* Wilson contended that "class has become more important than race in determining black life-chances in the modern industrial period; in the economic realm, . . . the black experience has moved historically from economic racial oppression experienced by virtually all blacks to economic subordination for the black underclass."[1]

A representative response to Wilson's thesis came from Charles V. Willie, who accused Wilson of adopting "the perspective of the dominant people of power" in using social class theory to explain poverty.

> *From the perspective of the dominant people of power, the social stratification system in the United States is open and anyone who has the capacity can rise within it. This orientation toward individual mobility tends to mask the presence of opportunities that are institutionally based such as attending the "right" school, seeking employment with the "right" company or firm, and being of the "right" race. Also, this orientation toward individual mobility tends to deny the presence of opposition and oppression that are connected with institutions. According to the perspective of the dominant people of power, opportunity, and especially educational and economic opportunity, is a function of merit.*[2]

In contention with Wilson, Willie stressed both that race and class formed a complex of interrelated characteristics and that all classes of Blacks still experience barriers to economic opportunity largely as a consequence of racial and sexual discrimination.

In response to Willie and other critics, Wilson reiterated in a subsequent revision of his book that he had not argued that race was irrelevant but that it was of relative importance. Wilson highlighted, in particular, the failure of public policy, such as civil rights legislation, and special racial programs, such as affirmative action, to address adequately the problems of the black underclass. Wilson remarked,

> I am convinced that the recent developments associated with our modern industrial society are largely responsible for the creation of a semi-permanent underclass in the ghettos, and that the predicament of the underclass cannot be satisfactorily addressed by the mere passage of civil rights laws or the introduction of special racial programs such as affirmative action. Indeed the very success of recent anti-discrimination efforts in removing racial barriers in the economic sector only points out, in sharper relief, other barriers which create greater problems for some members of the black population than for others, barriers which, in short, transcend the issue of racial ethnic discrimination and depict the universal problems of class subordination.[3]

Both Wilson and Willie raise significant issues that Blacks must keep in mind as we seek to understand our contemporary situation. On the one hand, because both are actually making arguments about the relationship between race and class (but from different perspectives), we are alerted to the increasingly stratified condition of Blacks that belies any monolithic description of black experience. On the other hand, their positions caution us against moving too quickly to propose a monolithic prescription for the alleviation of problems impeding black liberation. Considering both Wilson's and Willie's positions from my perspective as an ethicist concerned about black liberation, I propose that a critical reinterpretation of the race versus class debate discloses an ethical dilemma upon which the black community must reflect seriously if liberation is to be more than a utopian vision.

## A Critical Reinterpretation

To argue whether race or class is more determinative of black life chances today is to engage in a misleading debate. When black scholars seek to expose the greater impact and effects of race or class, they tend toward analyses of the oppression of Blacks that focus solely upon external factors—white racism or capitalist exploitation. Such analyses are limited, either emphasizing a trenchant critique of white racism or offering a single-factor solution, such as greater educational or employment opportunities.

However, if one argues that race and class are dialectical factors that have created a complex situation of black oppression, then the following two interrelated (yet distinguishable) issues come to the fore. First, maintaining a race-class dialectic of black oppression presses one to evaluate public policy designed to alleviate the oppression of Blacks. As Wilson points out, civil rights legislation and special racial programs such as affirmative action do not address adequately the problems of the black underclass.[4] Or, as Paula Giddings, a black journalist and historian, has expressed it, "The success of the civil rights movement, including anti-sex discrimination laws, has ensured that black men and women have de jure access to the political and economic mainstream. The key question now is: How do they become empowered once they get in?"[5]

Second, positing a race-class dialectic exposes the need to examine the meaning and/or role of class within the black community itself. Comments by some prominent Blacks during a discussion of the condition of the black middle class in the United States today reveal the need for such an examination. For example, Frank Mingo, president of Mingo-Jones Advertising, the second largest minority-owned communications company in the United States, contends that "Blacks have trouble talking about the issue of class. We don't like to discuss it. But class exists. I don't mean it in a derogatory way, but a black family that moves into a higher socioeconomic level inevitably develops a new and different social agenda."[6]

The divergent responses given to a question regarding the responsibility of the black middle class to the black underclass suggest the range of concerns that social stratification poses for Blacks. The responses range from primary responsibility (not relieving the federal government entirely but suggesting that the black middle class "be in the vanguard in terms of finding solutions"), to a need for the black middle class to "be willing to judge" the irresponsible behavior of the underclass, to the assertion that the first obligation of the black middle class is "to survive."[7]

Thus, it is critical for both debate and analysis that race and class are held in dialectical tension. By doing so, the limited understanding of black oppression premised upon a race versus class dichotomy is exposed, and the external and internal dimensions of such can be examined. The external dimension of black oppression refers to the way black life is circumscribed by white racism (race) and capitalist exploitation (class). Analyzing the political economy of black life leads to questions about what type(s) of public policy will best address continuing racial and economic injustices and lead to actual empowerment. The internal dimension forces us to consider how social stratification within the black community is a condition of and response to life in a racist context. Analyzing the internal dimension, we examine the meaning and role of class interests for Blacks ourselves in our development and execution of strategies for black liberation. Presupposing this interpretation of a dialectical tension between race and class that creates external and internal dimensions of black oppression, this book focuses upon the internal dimension.

It is my contention that by focusing upon the internal dimension of black oppression, the ethical dilemma deriving from social stratification within the black community can be brought to light. This is the case because black class structure can result in "the possible isolation of the upper classes from the lower ones. Wherever this has occurred, evidence seems to indicate that intensified stresses, strains, and intragroup conflicts have ensued. What makes the situation crucial is that it portends structural, organizational and philosophical divisions among groups who theoretically are bound together in the pursuit of a common goal."[8]

Evidence of the stresses, strains, and intragroup conflicts related to social stratification within the black community has been cited, even during the civil rights era of the sixties and into the seventies. For example, a case study of conflict over control of the NAACP in a mid-Atlantic city revealed "a conflict between two classes and their representatives in the Negro community, the 'old line' upper class and the upwardly mobile lower class." The study showed that the tension between the classes was also undergirded by the different philosophical and political strategies of the two classes. The upper class espoused "a kind of 'racial diplomacy'" that served to protect its favored position without threatening the racial status quo. The lower class exhibited a more aggressive and militant philosophy that promoted the concerns of the black masses. In the end, the upper class was pressed to consider whether it might regain "lost status by maximizing class or ethnic (racial) identity."[9] Similarly, when younger black militants accused older black middle-class civil rights leaders of lacking concern for lower-class Blacks, it led to alienation of some older leaders of the movement, resulting in a lapse in leadership.[10] Likewise, a study of the black middle class in 1971 described them as a group who sought isolation from both whites and lower-class Blacks; they sympathized but did not empathize with the black masses. In fact, in this study, the black middle class exhibited pervasive personal self-interest and conservatism with respect to racial protest.[11]

Interpretative and empirical studies on class perceptions and attitudes of black classes further support the assertion that social stratification fosters distress, if not divisiveness, among members of the black community. In a three-year study (1982–1985) of black college graduates that describes them as "a black elite," 90 percent identified themselves as middle class. When asked to evaluate the contribution of the black middle class to "the survival and advancement of the less fortunate black masses," a majority of this group criticized the relationship between more successful Blacks and the black masses, even expressing concern over "a growing, very serious alienation" between the two groups. Significant to this discussion is the fact that the group was of two minds about this predicament. On the one hand, they felt that they should do more to serve the black poor. On the other, they tended to blame the poor, "almost completely ignor[ing] injustices which are literally built into the American social system where racism, economic exploitation, and blatant inequalities are inherent in the black experience."[12]

More findings from recent studies are consistent with these earlier ones and bring forth additional issues that must be taken into account regarding the moral dilemma deriving from social stratification. For example, in a study seeking to investigate the actual relationship between lower-class Blacks and more successful Blacks relative to one another and whites, using demographic indicators of class status (for example, education, occupation, family income, and employment), the researcher found mixed data in support of growing social class polarization in the black community. In other words, there are some absolute measures by which different classes of Blacks can be interpreted as being polarized, but there are also relative measures that show us that we are close together with reference to larger societal factors.[13]

Furthermore, when the same researcher and others examined surveys of class perceptions and identification among Blacks, they found that Blacks perceive objective class divisions premised upon mental versus manual labor. This contradicts research and common understandings among black people that we are aware of prestige and status differences but do not exhibit class consciousness. Blacks tend to identify themselves more often as working class than middle class, although there is a sizable segment of the black population who have the socioeconomic indicators of middle class and perceive themselves as such.[14] Likewise, the "black underclass" reveals a grasp of the institutional constraints of race and class impinging upon them, and they have "ambivalent and complex" attitudes toward the "success" of the black middle class.[15]

Even more evident are contending moral, political, and economic ideologies underpinning the stances of black leaders and their strategies for addressing black oppression. An admittedly oversimplified typification of the contending positions is black liberalism and black conservatism. The black liberal position is represented by leadership of traditional and newer organizations, such as the NAACP and Rainbow Coalition, whose focus is primarily upon civil rights and greater social, political, and economic participation in U.S. society. The conservative position is represented by leadership of self-help organizations, such as the National Center for Neighborhood Enterprise.

Analyses by and of black intellectuals point out the following further characteristics of these two stances. Black liberalism emphasizes moral suasion and a reformist political agenda, including social policies such as integration and affirmative action. Black conservatism supports values clarification and political agendas such as opposition to affirmative action, abolition or lowering of adult minimum wage, proposals for enterprise zones in inner cities, and enormous cutbacks in social programs.[16]

Just as Wilson and Willie both contribute to our struggle to understand the complexity of black oppression today, black liberals and black conservatives in dialogue and tension will lead us to a more comprehensive response that may, in fact, be consistent with black liberation as an institutional and interpersonal reality. I am thus arguing that we must closely analyze social stratification within the black community because it represents the point at which Blacks have adopted this society's competitive class consciousness—its emphasis upon individual effort and competition over and against others—rather than develop a corporate race-class consciousness that would undergird the black liberative struggle. The assimilative acceptance of this competitive class consciousness on the part of Blacks has led, in effect, to the ethical dilemma of the internal dimension of black oppression: competitive individualism versus intragroup social responsibility.[17]

Two manifestations of this dilemma are false black consciousness and "sympathy without empathy." First, false black consciousness means that black people lack an awareness of one another as interrelated; in other words, they lack understanding of what the relationship between individual autonomy and communal autonomy should and might be for black people. All Blacks caught in this false black consciousness, but leaders in particular, do not promote the liberation of Blacks as a *group* from oppression in the United States. Second, there is "sympathy without empathy." Upper-class and middle-class Blacks may be willing emotionally and/or intellectually to advocate the plight of the lower classes but do not participate on behalf of or with lower classes of Blacks to effect mutual liberation. In fact, upper-class and middle-class Blacks entrapped by competitive class consciousness do not truly believe they are in need of liberation. This belief leads to isolation of the upper and middle classes from the lower classes and alienation of the lower classes from the upper and middle classes, creating disunity where *functional* unity is essential.

The dilemma of competitive individualism versus intragroup social responsibility within the black community is, therefore, a critical problem for ethical reflection. I will argue that communalism rather than liberal individualism is not only the means for resolving the ethical dilemma but is foundational for black liberation. Accordingly, the aim of this book is to propose intragroup social responsibility as the basis of a mediating ethic for black liberation and as a means for mediating between accommodative and aggressive political activism, between religious radicalism[18] for social change and the socioeconomics of societal change, between progress for individual Blacks and progress for Blacks as a group.[19]

Presupposing that this ethical dilemma has evolved throughout black history, I have focused my discussion in two primary ways. First, I describe the origin and evolution of this dilemma as a historical and sociological phenomenon during the nineteenth and early twentieth centuries. Second, I explore the insights of black women reformers within the club movement of the nineteenth century as a resource for formulating a mediating ethic. I examine the club movement because these reformers self-consciously addressed problems faced by stratified Blacks through efforts to "uplift" both black women and the entire race. This descriptive and critical analysis will lead to a normative proposal of a mediating ethic for black liberation.

# 3
# Roots of the Dilemma (1800–1920)

In this chapter, I discuss the origin and development of social stratification and the dilemma of competitive individualism versus intragroup social responsibility in the black community. The historical movements in black people's political and economic existence from the antebellum into the postbellum periods—slavery, emancipation, urbanization—serve as the general outline for this discussion. For each historical movement, I highlight historical and socioeconomic factors that were particularly conducive to the development of black social stratification, followed by an interpretation of race-class consciousness and ideologies for racial advancement operative among Blacks at that time. The goal is to reveal the relationship between the historical sources of black social stratification and the present ethical dilemma.

## Slavery: Historical, Social, and Economic Factors

By the nineteenth century, slavery was a major feature of the historical and socioeconomic context of the United States. Although the African slave trade was legally closed in 1808, illegal African trade, domestic slave trade, and slave breeding led to an increase in the slave population that further entrenched slavery. The total black population in the United States increased from 757,000 in 1790 to 4.4 million in 1860, and each census during the pre-Civil War period indicated that 86 percent or more of the Blacks were slaves.[1] The stratification that developed among the slave and free populations of Blacks during this era thus constitutes the first source of black stratification.

For the black slave population social stratification originated with the division of slave labor on the plantation. This consisted broadly of house servants, artisans, and field hands. Because the majority of slaves (both men and women) were field hands, the house servants and artisans might be described as an elite who were differentiated from the masses on the basis of the work they performed, the social advantages they obtained, and their relationships to the master.

House servants ("mammies," butlers, cooks, housemaids, coachmen) in the agricultural setting had, relatively speaking, more congenial labor. They also had better clothes, food, and sleeping quarters, were sometimes taught to read and write, and often were mulattoes with a blood tie to the master.

> Better cared for, often lighter in skin color, and certainly much closer to the seat of power, the house slave looked down on everyone except the 'quality' whites. Human, if not all too human, the colored domestics felt that they were far superior to other slaves. And they considered their jobs as sort of a family privilege to be passed down from father to son and mother to daughter.[2]

Likewise, artisans were skilled laborers (shoe or harness makers, carpenters, blacksmiths, cabinetmakers, seamstresses, tailors, etc.) whose trade made them beneficial to their masters in terms of earning power and their monetary value as property. Frequently, these slaves lived in towns and were hired out by their masters as well as engaged in self-hire; they maintained a more loosely supervised relationship with their masters.[3]

However, the fact that slaves participated in this division of labor does not explain fully the development of stratification among Blacks. The perceptions of slaves themselves as to status and social structure within the slave community is important for understanding stratification among the slave population. Whereas one must acknowledge the objective criteria for stratification derived from slavery as a labor system, one must also recognize that the slave population constituted a parallel community.[4]

As a parallel community, the slaves' perceptions of their social structure included awareness of distinctions premised upon the division of labor but were not limited by it. In fact, some evi-

dence suggests that the slaves rejected occupation as a sole criterion for high social standing within the community. Instead,

> occupations translated into high social standing only if they com-
> bined two of the following features: mobility (frequently allowing
> the slave to leave the plantation); freedom from constant supervi-
> sion by whites; opportunity to earn money; and provision of ser-
> vice to other blacks.[5]

These qualifications thus meant that house servants and artisans
were not automatically considered an elite group by the slaves;
they had to earn their position within the slave social structure:

> when house servants were able to walk that thin line between
> maintaining the appearance of loyalty to masters with the
> reality of serving their fellow blacks, they ranked high as indi-
> viduals in the black hierarchy.[6]

From the slaves' point of view, those at the top of their social
structure performed services for Blacks rather than whites. One
suggestive model of how slaves on the plantation divided themselves into classes places conjurors, physicians, midwives, and
preachers in an upper class; creators of material culture, verbal
artists, and self-employed slaves in a middle class; and ordinary
field hands, exploitative drivers, and live-in house servants with
long tenure in a lower class.[7] Urban slaves in southern cities
framed distinctions among themselves in terms of color, occupation, and the prominence of their masters.[8]

Along with stratification among the slave population, there
was stratification among the free Blacks.[9] Members of the free
black population were marginal persons in the antebellum period
both because of the challenge to slavery that their existence posed
and their varied origins (e.g., freed slaves, mulatto descendants
of white slaveholders, children of free colored persons, children
of free Negro and Indian parentage, indentured servants who
had completed their terms of service, immigrants, self-purchase
freedpersons).[10] Thus, the objective and subjective criteria of social stratification among free Blacks tended to reflect their place
in society relative to the slave system as well as their varied origins.

Objectively, social stratification among free Blacks derived in large part from ownership of property because this was an area, unlike most others in their lives, in which they were not constrained by legal restrictions. Although there were wide variations in different sections of the country, between 1830 and 1860 there was a 100 percent increase in the land holdings of free Blacks.[11] For example,

> by 1837, in New York city, [free Blacks] owned $1.4 million worth of taxable real estate and had $600,000 on deposit in savings banks. In Cincinnati, free Negro property was valued at more than $500,000. In North Carolina they owned $480,000 worth of real property and $564,000 of personal property in 1860. In Charleston, 352 free Negroes paid taxes in 1859 on property valued in excess of $778,000. Tennessee's free Negroes owned about $750,000 worth of real and personal property in 1860. [The free Negroes of New Orleans] owned more than $15 million worth of property in 1860.[12]

Occupation and income were also objective criteria at this time. Free Blacks and urban slaves had a virtual monopoly in the mechanical trades, especially in the South where less competition with white artisans existed. Even in the North, where free Blacks were confined largely to common labor and domestic service because of the animosity of white workers, free Blacks (particularly those who had white clientele) were often successful hotel owners, tavern keepers, caterers, barbers, and even independent entrepreneurs such as sailmakers and lumber merchants.[13] Occupational success sometimes led to affluence. Two excellent examples of this were "Jehu Jones, proprietor of one of Charleston's best hotels, [who] amassed a fortune of more than $40,000 and sent his son to Amherst" and "James Forten . . . of Philadelphia [who] became a sailmaker and accumulated a fortune of more than $100,000."[14]

Subjectively, free Blacks often developed social distinctions within their own ranks and/or assumed an attitude of disassociation from the slave population premised upon their varied origins, ownership of property, income, occupation, skin color, and education. For example, in New Orleans, distinctions were made between free blacks of predominantly or pure African descent and those of mixed French and Spanish origins.[15] Likewise, an attitude of disassociation from other Blacks was assumed by some northern free Blacks of mixed ancestry who had attained some formal education, were artisans, tradesmen, "the higher type of personal and domestic servants," and who maintained a decent standard of living.[16]

Generally, broad threefold class structures emerged within communities of free Blacks in both the South and North. In the South, this class structure generally consisted of an upper class—families with considerable property (including slaves) who boasted of either aristocratic white ancestry or the absence of a tradition of slavery; a middle class—substantial artisans with stable families and moderate incomes; and a lower class—persons with little skill and small incomes. A particularly interesting feature of the class structure among southern free blacks in some cities were the mulatto elites.

> *In Louisiana, Florida, and Mobile, elite free Negroes who were of French and Spanish origin emphasized their heritage and regarded other free Negroes with disdain. They established journals, wrote poetry in French, and sent their children to France for their education. Wealth and light-skin color were most often the distinguishing characteristics of the free Negro elite everywhere, although some exceptions existed. Publicly they often identified with white society and did not condemn slavery. . . .*[17]

In the North, class divisions among free Blacks were similar to those of the South, except for the upper stratum. The upper stratum in the North included independent artisans and businessmen, e.g., barbers, restaurateurs, caterers, tailors, and contractors, patronized by whites, and even domestic servants of the most socially prominent white families. There were also educated professional persons in law, teaching, medicine, and the ministry who were included as part of a northern elite.[18]

Thus, social stratification among Blacks during the slavery era consisted of one within the slave population and another within the free population. The basic features of both parallel systems were stratification based upon the black population's relationship to white society and an internal social structure based on Blacks' perceptions of class among themselves. However, in order to understand the significance of these two systems for the development of the ethical dilemma of competitive individualism versus intragroup responsibility, one must understand the caste-class structure of society during this era. In both the South and the North, Blacks as a group were regarded as inferior premised upon a racial ideology of the "black child/savage which served both caste and class functions."[19]

In the antebellum South, the caste function of the ideology of the black child/savage was blatantly evident on the plantation. Slaves were subjected to stratification based upon the division of labor not for economic efficiency alone but as a means of social control. Likewise, caste subordination operated significantly in the lives of free Blacks in the South through proscriptive policies such as a requirement to carry certificates of freedom, enslavement for petty debts or other legal infractions, disallowance of black testimony against white persons, subjection to slave curfews, prohibition against free assembly without white supervision, restricted interstate migration, and disfranchisement. Free Blacks in the North faced some of these same constraints and also had their economic progress restrained by policies such as ordinances against black labor in certain trades.[20]

The class function of the ideology in the South before the Civil War was related to class tensions between white slaveholders (who constituted only 5.5 percent of the white population in 1860) and nonslaveholding white workers; "a unique pattern of class conflict was taking shape in the Old South—white labor vs. the slaveholding class and their slave 'capital.'"[21] Thus, the ideology of the black child/savage was needed to perpetuate the superiority of whites as a group so that class tensions between whites were minimized by the notion of white caste superiority.[22] In the North, the ideology also served caste-class interests.

> *As it functioned within the northern society of the Market Revolution, the ideology of the 'child/savage' received considerable force from general white middle class fears of the new urban industrial society; it also reflected the particular class concerns of industrial employers and reinforced the degradation and control of industrial workers. As Irish immigrants crowded into growing cities and as America acquired an industrial proletariat, racial and class imagery often blurred together into a caste/class ideol-*

*ogy and intensified antiblack antagonism even in the virtually all-white society of the North.*[23]

Class tensions between white industrialists and other classes of whites were thus reduced when the racial ideology translated into a caste pattern in employment which relegated Blacks to the bottom of the occupational scale. For example, during the 1860s, as many as 87 percent of Blacks held menial jobs in New York and New Haven.[24]

### Race-Class Consciousness and Ideologies for Racial Advancement

Living under the ascription and proscription of caste-class subordination produced a mixed response on the part of Blacks. On the plantation, slaves responded by not accepting white standards of stratification as the sole criterion for social status and structure in the slave community. Yet, by establishing a social structure in contradistinction to white standards, the slaves granted legitimacy to stratification insofar as white standards served as a point of reference that led to tensions within the slave community (tensions that occasionally resulted in betrayal of plots to revolt). Some house servants were pretentious and had contempt for field slaves; some drivers adopted the social attitudes of their white masters and treated fellow slaves cruelly; some mulatto slaves thought themselves superior because of their mixed ancestry and sought exclusion from the rest of the slaves.[25] All slaves seemed to recognize that they lived in a society that measured the worth of an individual by standards of middle-class respectability.

Likewise, the legitimacy of white standards for stratification came forcefully into play as free Blacks responded to their marginality, and class lines between elite, middle, and lower classes developed. Although the cleavage along class lines was particularly evident in the South where a rigidity of caste discrimination was maintained in order to safeguard the institution of slavery, the "economics of marginality" allowed only a very few free Blacks to succeed in either the North or South, and many others were either just able to make a living or impoverished. A strained relationship between the free elite and the other classes of free Blacks derived then from the need of the former to secure a fragile position of privilege in relation to white society and the need of the latter to defend themselves against the animosity of both white society and the free elite.[26] Furthermore, free Blacks were caught by the intransigence of caste subordination even as they organized in response to it. The black convention movement, black participation in the abolition movement, and the formation of separate black communal institutions (such as benevolent, literary, masonic societies, and churches) illustrate variously an ambiguous defensive posture based in part upon a quest for mechanisms by which Blacks could develop and prove their worthiness for inclusion in society on middle-class terms.[27]

A continuum of contending strategies for racial advancement from nationalism to assimilationism suggests race-class conscious ideologies on the part of free Blacks. Blacks who proposed emigration or the creation of independent black states because of the impossibility of black political and economic advancement were clearly on the extreme nationalist end of the continuum, having concluded that neither inclusion on white middle-class terms nor reform of the capitalist United States was desirable or possible. In contrast, those who advocated assimilation (including miscegenation) apparently agreed with white society's racist and classist criteria for inclusion in the United States' version of democracy. Between the extremes, race-class ideology combined varying nationalist and assimilationist elements as Blacks fought for constitutional rights and socioeconomic opportunity as well as stressed their ethnicity through self-help activities aimed at fostering racial solidarity.[28]

For example, black nationalism during the decade previous to the Civil War has been described as a "religiopolitical" ideology infused with "assimilationist or acculturating tendencies" espoused by the black middle classes who sought to transmit Anglo-American values to the black community; some even used the term "Anglo-African" to describe themselves.[29] The use of the term Anglo-African, as well as other terms vying for acceptance in controversy over an acceptable name for the race, signaled class biases. Other terms vying for acceptance were "African" (used among Blacks in the North in organizational titles and among the masses, stressing African ancestry) and "colored" (advocated by wealthy black elites who wished to see interracial cooperation and the dissolution of separate black institutions or by ᵛ black leaders who wanted to avoid association with the negative stereotype of Africa).[30]

A mixed response on the part of enslaved and free Blacks during the slavery era revealed, in part, assimilative acceptance of social class as an indicator of one's place in society and, in part, adamant rejection of the idea that Blacks were a homogeneous inferior caste. From this mixed response arose the pattern for the current ethical dilemma: Blacks were living in a society that valued individualism and measured success in terms of individual striving and achievement; they were not perceived as individuals but as a subordinate group. They were thus caught between knowing what the society valued and the reality of their existence. Social stratification and competitive race-class consciousness of Blacks were consequences of the historical and economic dynamics of slavery and continued to evolve when slavery was abolished.

### Emancipation: Historical, Social, Economic Factors

Although the Thirteenth Amendment abolished slavery in 1865, the caste-class structure of the society remained intact. In one sense, social stratification among Blacks continued to operate within the parameters of caste subordination established during slavery; in another sense, sociopolitical and economic factors during Reconstruction facilitated transitions in black stratification, especially in the South.

Generally speaking, the broad division of Blacks between freedpersons (former slaves) and those who were free before the Civil War is key to understanding social stratification in the black community after emancipation. Those Blacks who were free before the war and had accumulated wealth, property, and education comprised disproportionately the upper class of the black community during the period immediately after emancipation.[31] In fact,

> *[t]he animosities inherited from the antebellum era festered and grew after the war. Fearful of being thrown together with the ragtag, destitute former slaves who were fleeing the plantations with little more than the clothes on their backs, some members of the elite retreated still further to themselves, cursed the general*

*Emancipation, and yearned for the old days. . . . Honing their*
*taste for the high life through education and travel, they seemed to*
*be preparing themselves for the moment they might be accepted*
*into the dominant part of the dominant caste. Although subject to*
*much of the same racial oppression that entrapped poorer blacks,*
*this "creme de la creme of the Southern light colored aristoc-*
*racy" rarely joined the movement for racial uplift. Instead, sus-*
*tained by the hope that class would prevail over race, they sought*
*to convince whites they were a caste apart from blacks, or, at least,*
*to renew the alliance with upper-class whites which had given*
*them their privileged position during the antebellum years.*[32]

At the same time, freedpersons were largely illiterate or semi-
literate former field slaves who were held in contempt by the
older class of free Blacks because they formed a lower class
within the black community.

*Many freed[persons] sensed the rejection of blacks implicit and*
*often explicit in the elite's exclusivist ways, and they returned it*
*at every opportunity. One Alabama Radical Republican expressed*
*the feelings of many newly liberated slaves when he blasted the old*
*light-skinned creole caste who, "inflated with pride at their sup-*
*posed superiority to 'common niggers,' have assumed such airs*
*that sensible people are heartily disgusted with them."*[33]

Cognizant of this elitist attitude on the part of some upper-class
free Blacks, freedpersons asserted their own class interests
through efforts to acquire land and education as the basis for re-
alizing socioeconomic emancipation for themselves.[34]

Initially, then, the social stratification of Blacks after emancipation may be described in terms of the broad socioeconomic and
political class divisions between those Blacks who were free persons before the Civil War and those who were former slaves.
However, this broad division does not offer a complete explana-
tion of the difference that freedom made in the social stratification of Blacks. Two other significant factors contributed to the
relationship between emancipation and the transitions in black
stratification which it precipitated.

First, many of the middle and lower classes of antebellum free
persons had ties with the former slaves through blood, marriage,

religious affiliation, and an attitude of alienation from whites. "Rather than feeling threatened by the general Emancipation, [these] free Blacks saw only new opportunities to assert their leadership, strengthen African churches, and achieve the equality they had long desired."[35] These free Blacks and freed slaves formed a political bloc with which the colored (mulatto) elite had to contend in order to protect their class interests. In terms of overall black stratification, this sociopolitical bloc represented the roots of a mechanism for class mobility whereby greater class differentiation among Blacks might become feasible. This was the case because this bloc worked to procure legislation that would improve and/or provide services for Blacks, such as education, whereby *all* Blacks might have become better prepared, thus enabling socioeconomic progress.

Second, inasmuch as emancipation imposed the crucial task of integrating approximately four million freed slaves into U.S. society and economy, the federal government had to initiate Reconstruction measures, such as the Freedman's Bureau (1866). The bureau issued rations (to both Blacks and dislocated poor whites), operated hospitals, supervised contracts between freedpersons and their employers, assisted in the education of freedpersons, and leased or sold some abandoned and confiscated lands to freedpersons. The work of the Bureau in the area of education was especially successful. When the Freedman's Bureau (along with northern philanthropists, missionaries, and black religious organizations) opened a variety of schools, freedpersons took advantage of the opportunity to such an extent that the literacy rate among Blacks increased from 19 percent in 1870 to 56 percent in 1890.[36] Although the Bureau's efforts for the redistribution of confiscated lands were not so far-reaching, when public lands were opened to settlers (Black or white) under the Southern Homestead Act of 1866 in Alabama, Mississippi, Louisiana, Arkansas, and Florida, some 4,000 Blacks succeeded in becoming property owners.[37] Thus, Reconstruction measures fostered greater accessibility for all Blacks to these two critical factors of social stratification among Blacks: education and property ownership. Greater accessibility to these factors of social stratification earmarked a transition whereby freedpersons were enabled to compete with antebellum free Blacks with respect to educational and economic attainment. In sum, the alliance of middle and

lower classes of free Blacks with former slaves as well as the gov-
ernmental Reconstruction measures were instrumental in alter-
ing the structure of black stratification and made it a more open
class system wherein both greater mobility and increased differentiation might occur.

Still, these transitions in black stratification cannot be assessed
apart from the continuing caste-class structure of society as well
as the class issues between southern and northern whites at the
time. During the period referred to as Radical Reconstruction
(1866–1877), class issues between southern and northern whites
were particularly acute because of the same political and economic changes fostering social and economic mobility among
Blacks.[38]

First, because Reconstruction governments in the South represented a coalition between northern industrial capitalists, black
labor, and radicals in the Republican party, their legislative
actions (enfranchisement of ex-slaves and disfranchisement of
many leading southern whites, heavy taxation of large property
owners, the repeal of some black codes) threatened to displace
permanently the planter elite in the South. Second, services (e.g.,
a free public-school system) instituted by Reconstruction governments were generally favorable to both the black and white lower
classes. Third, the scarcity and determination of black labor
(some former slaves refused to work in agriculture and others refused to work under conditions akin to slavery) and the rise of
independent merchants (financed largely by northern capital)
contributed to economic hardship for the planter class.[39]

Confronted by these shifts in political and economic power, the
planter class adopted an economic and political strategy of their
own. They became a "new merchant-landlord class" that used
"white supremacy" and "home rule" as political rhetoric to re-
capture the loyalty of lower-class whites who had also benefited
from Reconstruction governments.[40] That is, an emphasis on the
racial division between Blacks and whites was again used to dis-
courage class divisions among whites. The aim was to get all
whites, regardless of class, to focus on race differences. Consequently, Radical Reconstruction was overthrown through a combination of extralegal means (particularly the use of intimidation
and terror by the Klan), an alliance of southern Conservatives

and moderate Republicans that defeated the Radical Republicans in every southern state by the late 1870s, an escalating struggle between black labor and northern industrial capitalism which had less and less need for the initial coalition, and the Compromise of 1877 (an agreement having mutually beneficial political and economic ramifications for both the South and the North).[41]

With the collapse of Reconstruction, the racial ideology of white superiority–black inferiority manifested a twofold caste-class function. The merchant-landlord class sought to solve the South's labor problem by removing Blacks from political power so as to force them into economic subservience. The aim was to recreate a "controlled labor force" akin to that of slavery. The continuance of the "black child/savage" ideology was evident as whites (across class lines) engaged in and/or supported the terrorism of the Klan to suppress Blacks, while some upper-class whites offered "protection" (another form of paternalism) to those Blacks who were willing to stay in their "place."[42] This paternalism by some upper-class whites also served to play Blacks against lower-class whites.

In the North, an ever-present fear of "invasion" by Blacks following emancipation and a need to stabilize economic relations with the South were the dubious motives for northern involvement in Reconstruction. These motives undergirded racial ideology and its caste-class consequences in the North. The fear of invasion was premised upon the disdain of whites for social equality with Blacks and immigrant labor's trepidation about the competition of Blacks for jobs. Blacks in the North were, in turn, relegated to menial places within the industrial economy and were the object of immigrant violence.[43] Moreover, the consequences of the North's racial ideology were apparent in the South in that, along with the beneficial outcomes (i.e., education) of the Freedman's Bureau, the Bureau also promoted a system of contract labor that nullified the freedpersons' right to establish the conditions under which they would labor, effectively obstructing their efforts to become economically independent. The Bureau was supposed to enforce mutually binding contracts between freedpersons and planters. However, although the Bureau moralized to the ex-slaves about proving themselves worthy of freedom by honoring the contracts and even used measures, such as cutting rations to Blacks in refugee camps and enforcing vagrancy laws to force compliance, planters were infrequently subject to penalty for not honoring the terms of contracts.[44]

The demise of Reconstruction thus rendered the black masses subject to a "reconstruction of black servitude."[45] Although the revival of black codes, displacement from many skilled trades, increased lynching, and diminishing appropriations for black schools in the South effected the lives of all Blacks, these caste-class restrictions, along with others such as convict leasing and sharecropping, had a disproportionate impact upon those who were recently freed slaves. For example, the ex-slaves' quest for economic emancipation through land ownership was critically affected. In Mississippi, a black code outlawed the selling or leasing of land to Blacks, and some ex-slaves who had managed to acquire land had it seized as the federal government returned land to pardoned ex-Confederate landowners.[46]

In summary, the emancipation period was a time when historical and economic factors (especially during Reconstruction) combined to facilitate transitions in black stratification in the South. The two systems of parallel stratification that had existed during slavery merged into a more open system wherein both greater mobility and increased differentiation might occur. However, by 1877 the conditions that had facilitated the transitions were undercut, demonstrating the contingency of black stratification within the caste-class structure of the society as a whole. Although the ambivalent effects of Reconstruction upon black progress may have produced a desire on the part of Blacks to reevaluate their relationship to that caste-class structure, the mixed black response (in part, assimilative acceptance of social class as an indicator of one's place in society and, in part, adamant rejection of the caste status of Blacks), which had emerged during slavery, prevailed.

### Race-Class Consciousness and Ideologies for Racial Advancement

The broad division between former slaves and antebellum free Blacks serves also as a basis for understanding differences in the race-class consciousness of Blacks and ideologies for racial advancement during the emancipation period. As stated previously, the antebellum free mulatto elite comprised disproportionately the socioeconomic and political elite of the black community at this time. This group was not interested in any fundamental restructuring of society, such as the massive redistribution of land in the South, for they were seeking to remove obstacles to inclusion that racial caste subordination denied them but which their status should have afforded them. "If the mass of newly liberated slaves wanted economic, political, and social equality, in that order, the priorities of the black elite—composed disproportionately of free Negroes—were precisely the opposite."[47]

Some significant evidence of the class-based agenda of antebellum free elite as different from that of newly freed slaves is found in their political positions during Reconstruction. For example, correlations between the origins of black leaders in South Carolina[48] (a state with a distinct black majority and strong black Republican political leadership) and their sociopolitical stances is informative. During the debates of the constitutional convention in 1868, some interesting voting patterns among the black delegation came to the fore. On the issue of disfranchisement of former Confederates, freeborn and mulatto delegates favored moderation whereas slave-born and black delegates favored disfranchisement. The former wanted to establish that their motivations were conciliatory rather than punitive, reflecting their previous ties with the white ruling elite from whom some had acquired their freedom and/or initial socioeconomic advantages. Similarly, ardent support for a motion to have literacy and poll tax requirements for suffrage was offered by some freeborn mulattoes because of their status as educated and propertied individuals.[49]

In light of the predominance of antebellum free Blacks in the political arena, it is not surprising that the prevalent political philosophy during Reconstruction stressed a broad-based program for racial advancement derived from U.S. egalitarian traditions. "Negroes focused their attention upon becoming full-fledged citizens. The franchise, education, guarantees for civil rights, the acquisition of property and wealth, and the cultivation of morality were all designed to elevate Negroes and achieve integration into American society."[50]

Along with political divisions premised upon differing class

interests, there was "a growing cultural cleavage between un-
schooled rural Blacks and assimilated individuals [which] con-
fused intraracial and interracial relations for the rest of the
century."[51] This cleavage was indicative of the ambiguous contribution of education to the evolving race-class consciousness of
Blacks. As freed slaves attained education, they acquired not
only a means of socioeconomic mobility but also classist Anglo-
American culture and values.[52]

The post-Reconstruction period saw a continuance of the
group-name controversy. Many former slaves wished to be designated African whereas some black leaders discouraged the use
of African as a group name and in the titles of black organizations. These particular leaders—"no doubt concentrated mainly
among more privileged elements"—were concerned that the use
of the term "African" contributed to discriminatory practices and
also kept Blacks mindful of their slave past when the emphasis
should be upon inclusion in U.S. society.[53]

With emancipation, the race-class consciousness of Blacks and
their ideologies for racial advancement continued along lines that
originated during slavery. Competitive rather than corporate
race consciousness among the antebellum free elite was heightened by the actual and potential loss of economic advantage for
them as a class after emancipation. Because many educated antebellum free Blacks had been indoctrinated with a competitive
class consciousness, the prevailing race-class ideology for racial
advancement tended to accentuate the egalitarian U.S. traditions
(full citizenship rights) and de-emphasize racial group solidarity
as Africans (fearing that such encouraged discrimination and
mitigated against integration). These concerns reflected an elitist
point of view that separated black leadership from the masses of
former slaves. At the same time, as the former slaves began to
attain means for socioeconomic mobility through education, nurturance of their competitive class consciousness was also under-
way. Thus, emancipation represented a phase wherein the roots
of the present ethical dilemma of competitive individualism versus intragroup social responsibility were further entrenched. It
took an accelerated growth in black migration to both southern
and northern cities—an urbanization of the black populace—
before the class lines of black stratification as well as the parameters of the mixed black response began to shift.

## Urbanization: Historic and Economic Factors

Even before the deteriorating conditions of the post-Reconstruction period, some Blacks migrated to southern and northern cities immediately upon emancipation. In fact, some of the reasons given by Blacks for their earlier post-war migration foreshadowed those for post-Reconstruction migration: a desire to escape their bonds to the land and the control of former masters, fear of reprisals by whites who refused to accept the new status of Blacks, inadequate or nonpayment of wages, and the services that cities offered—superior schools, welfare agencies, and public relief.[54] The immediate post-war migrants, subsequent post-Reconstruction migrants, and the urban populations of those Blacks who were free prior to the Civil War comprise the chief protagonists during the urbanization period. Whereas transitions in black stratification during the immediate emancipation period occurred primarily in the South, urbanization characterizes that period in black history when the consequences of emancipation for Blacks in both the South and the North converge.

Immediately following the Civil War, interstate migration within the South was common among freed slaves. They sought areas where Blacks were the predominant group and there was a demand for black labor, for they reasoned that there was security in numbers. The crucial rationale among the freed slaves who moved into the cities and towns was that there "freedom was free-er." What they meant by this was that they expected to live "much easier" in the cities and towns because there they could find the protection of federal troops and employment opportunities other than agricultural labor as well as the camaraderie of other Blacks. Although their expectation of a "much easier" life was not fulfilled for many, migration to cities and towns continued because personal satisfaction ("a more meaningful and satisfying way of life"), if not great material prosperity, was attained by some.[55]

The migration had three major outcomes. First, the rural black migrants became largely part of a class of unskilled laborers, even if they had been slave artisans, either because of white prejudice whereby they were denied access to skilled jobs or because of the specialized skills required by an urban labor market. Second, those freed slaves who were successful in business (mostly as self-employed merchants) held a tenuous place within the southern urban economy because their services were often limited to black clientele who were poor themselves and they lacked both experience and finances. Third, those urban Blacks who had been free prior to emancipation found that their lives were becoming unduly restricted with the growth of the urban black population.[56]

These divisions, then, signified lines of social stratification among urban southern Blacks. In cities such as Atlanta, Montgomery, Nashville, Raleigh, and Richmond, black elites tended to center their lives in particular churches, educational institutions, and social clubs. For example, in Atlanta, the black elite was concentrated in the First Congregational Church, Atlanta University, and a dozen social clubs. At the other extreme, life for the black lower class in the cities was centered frequently in gambling and whiskey dens.[57] The disparate living conditions and residential location of the black elite and lower classes also reinforced the social distance between the classes. Typically, the migrant lower classes lived in overcrowded, minimally furnished housing under conditions not dissimilar to poor whites. Members of the black elite and middle classes often resided in neighborhoods with or in proximity to whites of a similar status. It is around 1890, as the numbers of Blacks in the southern cities and towns increased considerably, when the ability of the black elite to maintain their social distance from lower classes of Blacks with respect to matters such as residential location began to erode; separate black and white neighborhoods began to predominate in the urban setting at that time.[58]

Also, a developing middle class of business and professional persons as well as a class of "hardworking petty tradesmen, artisans, and laborers" were distinct components of southern urban black stratification. The middle class consisted mostly of successful former slaves who had earned property and wealth, thus providing their children with "the advantages of higher education and a secure economic base." The working class (just below this middle class) frequently owned their homes and enjoyed a relatively comfortable life. Still, though,

> for the majority of urban Negroes . . . the first twenty-five years
> after the war were years of frustration and disappointment. The

*year 1890 found them at the lowest levels of the economic ladder with little prospect of improvement. . . . The lack of economic power served to undermine the strength of blacks in warding off the discrimination generated by the white community.*[59]

Next, the migration of Blacks beyond the South proceeded in two directions. First, there were westward and northward migrations, termed "Exoduses"; the "Exodus of 1879" out of Tennessee led by "Pap" Singleton to Kansas is the premier example of this phenomenon.[60] Second, migrants settled in northern industrial cities. While the westward migration of Blacks is an important aspect of the migratory distribution of the black population during the post-Reconstruction period, this discussion focuses upon the greater migration to northern cities.

As stated previously, some black migration to northern cities occurred shortly after emancipation. However, northern migration began in earnest with the worsening conditions for Blacks by the last decade of the nineteenth century.

*The 1890s sounded several loud warnings of the collapse of black prospects in America. The three shrillest were Booker T. Washington's abnegation of black equality in his Atlanta Exposition speech of 1895; the U.S. Supreme Court's blessing on Jim Crow in its Plessy v. Ferguson decision of 1896; and the total eclipse by 1898 of the Populist movement with the resurgence of the solid Democratic South.*[61]

The northward migration of Blacks was thus well under way by 1900 and escalated after 1910 and during the years of the World Wars. "According to various contemporaneous estimates, between 1890 and 1910 around 200,000 black Southerners fled to the North; and between 1910 and 1920 another 300,000 to 1,000,000 followed."[62] The need for labor during the war years made initially feasible successful black migration to the North. During the war years, wages for Blacks in northern industrial cities could be as much as 400 percent higher than in the South.[63]

The influx of black migrants, however, was not without consequence. Indeed, black northern migration produced outcomes similar to those that occurred in the South. They largely became part of a lower class (factory or domestic workers), had restricted access to skilled jobs, professions, and business, and adversely affected the lives of those Blacks who already lived in the North.

As the numbers of black migrants increased, the black population of the North became entrapped in ghettoes, and this influenced negatively black stratification. For example, in Philadelphia's Seventh Ward, where free Blacks had resided before the Civil War, the arrival of southern black migrants aggravated tensions and created hostile conditions (particularly, an increase in crime) that were rooted in the socioeconomic disparity between classes of Blacks.[64] Also, stratification in the cities was manifested within the black community's social institutions. For instance, in Detroit "patterns of black social interaction reflected the class divisions in the community." Church membership is informative in this regard; congregants in white churches were among the elite of the black community, most black Methodists were middle class, and working- and lower-class Blacks attended the Baptist church.[65]

An equally significant effect of black northern migration and urbanization was the rise of a new elite that would displace and yet foster some ties with the old mulatto elite. By the 1920s, the new black elite in cities such as Detroit, Chicago, and Cleveland was no longer comprised of nonprofessionals (such as headwaiters in expensive downtown white restaurants or barbers with wealthy white clientele). The members of the new black elite were dependent on the patronage of black rather than white clientele. However, the new black elite frequently forged ties with the old mulatto elite through marriage; black men felt that marrying light-skinned women enhanced their social status.[66]

Florette Henri described the key differences between the new black and the old mulatto elites:

> *The new black elite that emerged as the migration went on consisted chiefly of self-made Negroes, black and light. . . . The people who made their living in business, banking, and real estate could not afford to separate themselves from the ghetto community on which they depended for support; they had to identify with lower-class people. Nor were old family and inherited wealth the values of other newly successful blacks, many of whom were artists and athletes. And the leaders who were the philosophers and organizers of new roles for black Americans rejected the old elite's doc-*

*trine of discreet advance through one's own efforts only, insisting rather on equality through legal and social reforms of the entire society.*[67]

Furthermore, the larger society was affected by and responded to the migration and urbanization of Blacks. In the South, whites grew concerned as their cheap labor began diminishing with the migration of Blacks from the region. Some southern states and cities enacted licensing laws and ordinances and levied fines to undercut the work of labor agents who were recruiting black workers for northern industry. In fact, "force was not infrequently used to prevent the taking of blacks North.... Labor agents were arrested. Trains carrying migrants were stopped, the blacks forced to return, and the agents beaten. Blacks might be terrorized or lynched on suspicion of trying to leave the state."[68]

This reaction by white southerners derive from these two poles of southern racial ideology. First, there was "a new paternalism" espoused by a new white middle class whose urban industrial interests set them apart from the old planter aristocracy. This "new paternalism" to which both Blacks and poor whites were subject was an elitism premised upon the right of character, intelligence, and property to rule, along with an attitude of benevolence (even supporting industrial education for the working classes) so as to promote economic progress (i.e., northern investment) in the "new South." Second, there was a belief that Blacks must be contained because black progress was a prelude to increasing racial antagonism. From this point of view, whites believed themselves in a competition for racial supremacy, and extinction rather than containment of Blacks was desirable.[69]

When these poles of southern racial ideology converged at the turn of the century, Darwinism provided the rationale for a conflictual perspective on race relations. The result was "Negrophobia," accentuating the "Negro as savage/beast" aspect of the Black-as-child/savage racial ideology operative during the slavery era.[70] Allegations of the rise of crime and increased sexual immorality (leading to assaults on white women) on the part of Blacks were asserted along with the application of Darwinian concepts of racial degeneracy and extinction in reference to the evolution of the black race.

Interestingly, the rise of the Populists during the 1890s was a further catalyst for the ascendancy of the competitive pole of southern racial ideology. The Populists, by uniting poor white and black farmers, threatened both race relations and the class position of upper-classes whites with urban industrial interests. These upper-class whites responded by arousing the fear of "Negro domination" and the end of white supremacy so as to reaffirm racial solidarity among whites. The combination of racial Darwinism and the economic threat from a coalition of black and white poor people culminated in the South's most severe racial discrimination and violent aggression through both legal (Jim Crow laws and disfranchisement) and extralegal (lynching and riots) means.[71]

Although there was also a southern Progressive white response during this period which may described as "accommodationist racism," its effect was minimal within the southern context but influential with respect to the North's response to the South and northern racial ideology.[72] That is, northerners were able to adopt an attitude of noninterference in southern affairs as they endorsed southern moderates who were concerned with uplifting and training a childlike race of Blacks. Indeed, southern and northern Progressives formed a kind of national consensus on race relations—one that supported the view that Blacks were inferior but should experience limited forms of social betterment, such as industrial education and the right to vote based upon literacy requirements, so as to promote social order.[73]

Furthermore, in the North, the persistence of a racial industrial caste system that relegated Blacks to the bottom of the occupational pyramid evidenced northern complicity in the racial ideology of black inferiority. Blacks were barred from joining white unions but were frequently used as strikebreakers, leading to increased violence between Blacks and immigrants. This violence occurred even though both groups were actually subject to the machinations of white supremacy—i.e., race prejudice and nativism, respectively. Likewise, the ghettoization of Blacks signified the level of white animosity as *de facto* residential segregation became the norm.[74]

In as much as changes in black social stratification during the urbanization period were the fruits of a more open class system in the black community initiated during the emancipation period, social stratification among Blacks began to have similar characteristics in both the South and the North. An emergent "self-made" black elite and middle class began to displace the old mulatto elite in both the South and North. This new elite and middle class relied on the black community to support their businesses and them as professionals. Finally, as Blacks across the country experienced more acutely white racist enmity, the mixed black response to the U.S. caste-class structure was strained and a heightened race-class consciousness created an interesting interplay between integrationist and nationalist elements within ideologies for racial advancement.

## Race-Class Consciousness and Racial Advancement Ideologies

The heightened race-class consciousness of Blacks that accompanied urbanization derived from their greater awareness of the virulence of caste-class oppression in U.S. society. The stark reality of the collusion of southern and northern white power elites in ending Reconstruction could not be ignored by Blacks of any class. As the ramifications of this collusion intensified by the final decade of the nineteenth century, it was clear that the terms for the inclusion of Blacks in U.S. society were not necessarily to be found within a broad-based approach to attain civil and political rights.

Instead of a broad-based approach, there were accomodationist/integrationist and protest/nationalist ideologies for racial advancement that utilized racial solidarity, self-help, and group economy as strategies for economic and moral development.[75] However, the race-class consciousness of proponents of each ideology revealed particular class biases. An interpretation of the Booker T. Washington–W. E. B. DuBois debate during this time will illustrate this point.

On the one hand, a "theory of social rehabilitation" was the basis for a primarily accommodative/integrationist ideology for racial advancement espoused by Booker T. Washington and others. Because of Washington's basic acceptance of the U.S. capitalist system, he desired to prepare Blacks for inclusion within that system; black development was to be "a normal part of national economic growth. . . . By combining a pedagogy to build individual self-confidence through the inculcation of skills with an ideology that emphasized capital accumulation, Washington provided an image of Blacks entering the modern economy through the tactic of separate enterprise."[76]

Insofar as Washington's ideology for racial advancement was one that might "unite rural freedmen and an urban bourgeoisie" by using the latter to train the former in separate black institutions, Washington and others manifested the racial solidarity of black nationalism. Yet, because the training of individual farmers and entrepreneurs was the priority, the proponents of this ideology were predominantly accommodative/integrationist, promoting competitive race-class consciousness.

On the other hand, a theory of "cultural revitalization" proposed by W. E. B. DuBois and others was predominately a protest/nationalist ideology. Here the nationalist feature came to the fore as DuBois highlighted the cultural distinctiveness of Blacks and asserted that Blacks' acceptance and appreciation of their heritage—black self-understanding—was prerequisite for economic and political achievement. This theory also bolstered "a new political ideology of nonpartisanship" and recognized the barriers imposed by the caste-class system upon the psychological and material well-being of Blacks.[77] Insofar as this theory did not actually promote the eradication of the capitalist system but encouraged a black reform movement led by a college-educated elite (DuBois's "Talented Tenth"), it had integrationist overtones. Still, though, because the theory does maintain the primacy of black ethnicity, its proponents had a corporate race-class consciousness as the basis of an ideology for racial advancement.

The continuing debate over a group name followed the lines of these ideologies. "From the late 1880s down to the opening years of the new century, the term *Afro-American*, frequently used, easily competed with *Negro* as the most popular designation for black people."[78] "Afro-American" was adopted largely by those in the protest/nationalist camp; "Negro" by those in the accommodative/integrationist.

In summary, during urbanization in the late nineteenth and early twentieth centuries, the mixed black response which began in slavery was exacerbated by hardening caste-class oppression. Race-class consciousness and ideologies for racial advancement among Blacks revealed attentiveness to economic and moral development as key for overcoming oppression. Yet, although the concepts of racial solidarity and self-help were part of ideologies for racial advancement, the overall aim was acceptance on the terms of white middle-class respectability.

This discussion reveals that from slavery through urbanization, Blacks had to decide on what terms, if any, inclusion in U.S. society was feasible and desirable. By buying into the overall system of social stratification, tensions between classes of Blacks produced different agendas for racial advancement. This situation mitigated against Blacks' perceiving their collective predicament. Thus, by the period of urbanization, Blacks were clearly mired in the dilemma of competitive individualism versus intragroup social responsibility—the dilemma of how to be a community in solidarity against racist, classist oppression. How black women in the late nineteenth and early twentieth centuries faced this dilemma is the subject of the next chapter.

# 4

# Black Women's Perspective on the Dilemma

The intent of this chapter is to depict the collective race-gender-class consciousness of black women during the nineteenth and early twentieth centuries. This serves as the basis for understanding the thought and work of the black women's club movement as a paradigmatic response to the dilemma of social stratification. This discussion is organized into three parts: (1) a sociohistorical and economic description of black women's lives in the nineteenth and early twentieth centuries; (2) an explication of "black women's perspective," their race-gender-class consciousness, through an examination of the writings of women from diverse walks of life; and (3) the response generated by that perspective as exhibited in the thought and work of the club movement.

## Social, Historical, and Economic Conditions

In the nineteenth century, all women's lives were circumscribed by the "cult of true womanhood or cult of domesticity." Women were to be wives and mothers who possessed the attributes of domesticity, submissiveness, piety, and purity. In effect, it perpetrated a classist and racist ideology of womanhood.

> *The parameters of the ideological discourse of true womanhood were bound by a shared social understanding that external physical appearance reflected internal qualities of character and therefore provided an easily discernible indicator of the function of a female of the human species: men associated "the idea of female softness and delicacy with a correspondent delicacy of constitution." . . . It is worth considering that a delicate constitution was*

*an indicator of class as well as racial position; woman as orna-*
*ment was a social sign of achieved wealth, while physical strength*
*was necessary for the survival of women in the cotton fields, in the*
*factories, or on the frontier.*[1]

Upper-class white women of leisure were best able to maintain
some semblance of this ideal of womanhood, and white middle-
class women sought to align their behavior with the "cult" as a
vehicle for social mobility. Working-class women and all black
women were considered to have transgressed the "cult." In fact,
working-class women and all black women were considered to
be freely available for sexual use by upper-class white males.

Industrialization during the eighteenth century which had
moved manufacture from the home into the factory combined
with the cult of true womanhood in the nineteenth century to
produce significant ramifications for women's lives. Most important, "this segregation create[d] a hardship both by demoting
female productivity within the home to a nonstatus and by con-
signing female labor in the market economy to an equally abys-
mal devaluation."[2]

Consequently, slave and free black women were bound together as a distinct group by oppression perpetrated by the rein-
forcing ideologies of the "cult of true womanhood" and white
racial superiority. Although both white and black women during
the nineteenth century were constrained by the "cult," there
were two radically different means by which gender oppression
operated in their lives: debasement for black women, idealization
for white women. Likewise, although both black women and
men experienced an equality in common oppression deriving
from life in a racist society, black women experienced racism in a
qualitatively different manner because of the additional constraints of sexism.

During the slavery era, the difference for black women
emerged from the interaction of race, gender, and class dynamics
revealed in their experience. Although the majority of women
and men were field hands rather than part of the elite (house servants and artisans) on the plantation, any class division between
female field hands and house servants was tempered by a
gender-specific norm of expediency. Slaveowners sometimes
treated black women as genderless and other times repressed

them in ways suited only for women: "the master took a more crudely opportunistic approach toward the labor of slave women, revealing the interaction between notions of women *qua* equal black workers and women *qua* unequal reproducers...."[3] Slave women who were pregnant or mothers with infant children were not exempted from work. All women were at risk of sexual exploitation, which was used as a form of punishment, as a means for the further economic exploitation of the slave woman (i.e., using her reproductive capacity to replenish and increase the domestic slave population), and as a mechanism to terrorize slave women so as to deter them from engaging in acts of resistance to overthrow the slave system.[4]

Furthermore, for slave women, the racial ideology of the black child/savage was complicated by the ideology of true womanhood such that social myths peculiar to black womanhood resulted. The social myths of Jezebel and Mammy were used to describe and proscribe black womanhood in slavery; the former stood as a counter-image (a woman controlled almost completely by her libido) and the latter as a blackened version of the true woman (surrogate mistress and mother).

> *The myth of Jezebel excused miscegenation, the sexual exploitation of black women, and the mulatto population. It could not, however, calm Southern fears of moral slippage and "mongrelization," or man's fear of woman's emasculating sexual powers. But the Mammy image could. Mammy helped endorse the service of black women in Southern households, as well as the close contact between whites and blacks that such service demanded. Together Jezebel and Mammy did a lot of explaining and soothed many a troubled conscience.*[5]

Likewise, the negative force of racial and gender ideologies undergirded the lack of economic opportunities for free black women. Free northern black women in the cities were disproportionately employed in domestic service which was associated with low pay, hard work, low prestige, and also carried the risk of sexual harassment by their employers' husbands.

> *By 1847, the majority of black Philadelphia women were washerwomen and domestic servants, numbering 2,085 of a total*

*black female population of 4,249. In addition, there were 486 black
needlewomen and 213 involved in some sort of trade. These trades
included dressmaking and hairdressing, jobs that were usually
performed in the home.*[6]

Because the work force in northern factories was overwhelmingly
female at the time, the employment situation of free black
women is a particularly telling example of the way in which gender and racial ideologies intertwined and had material consequences.

When free black women were able to attain professional cre-
dentials, they were either denied work in their profession or still
restricted economically and subjected to the indignities of racial
and sexual discrimination. Black teachers found that teaching positions were limited to the black community which could barely
(if at all) afford their services; some teachers found that they had
to perform domestic work in order to survive. When black
women lecturers traveled, they had to endure segregated accom-
modations for lodging and travel that would never have been acceptable for whites in general and white women in particular. As
Catherine Clinton has written, "In or out of slavery, black women
were confronted by the irony of their status within a culture
which celebrated a feminine model of domestic gentility."[7]

Both slave and free black women responded during the slavery
era to the overwhelming denigration of black womanhood along
a continuum of overt to covert resistance. Slave women were
leaders of and participants in slave revolts, led groups of fugitive
slaves to freedom, poisoned masters and set fires to masters'
homes, and sued for their rights to be free. According to Hine and
Wittenstein, slave women engaged in "three intimately related
forms of resistance" to their economic and sexual oppression:
sexual abstinence, abortion, and infanticide.[8] Free women participated in and/or organized societies that addressed the issues af-
fecting their lives. They were leaders and members of abolition
and women's rights groups, such as the National Female Anti-
slavery Society, and formed literary, educational, and mutual aid
societies, such as the Afric [sic] American Female Intelligence Society of Boston, the Ohio Ladies Education Society, and the New
Orleans' Colored Female Benevolent Society of Louisiana.[9]

Emancipation did not eradicate the ironic status of black

women; but, in seeking to actualize their freedom, black women shifted the parameters of that status. In the South, most black women (singly, with a spouse, or with female partners) continued to work primarily in agriculture as sharecroppers and tenant farmers or farm laborers hired out under the convict lease system. Others refused to work in the fields at all or at least under white supervision. Those who refused fieldwork were sarcastically referred to as "playing the lady," since it was incomprehensible that black women could fulfill standards of "true womanhood." However, as Jacqueline Jones has observed, this behavior on the part of recently emancipated black women did not represent an attempt to imitate white middle-class standards for women's roles.

> *In fact, . . . the situation was a good deal more complicated. First, the reorganization of female labor resulted from choices made by both men and women. Second, it is inaccurate to speak of the "removal" of women from the agricultural work force. Many were no longer working for a white overseer, but they continued to pick cotton, laboring according to the needs and priorities established by their own families.*[10]

Likewise in the North, black working-class women continued to experience economic hardship because of the racist-sexist terms under which their employment occurred. They continued to be confined largely to domestic service, and this meant that black women were disproportionately found within the lower socioeconomic ranks within the black community and the society at large.

Accordingly, black women contended against forces which conspired to undercut their freedom. Black women were a potent political presence during Reconstruction. For example, in South Carolina black women attended Republican meetings, guarded the weapons stacked behind the speaker's platform at political rallies, "applied the sanctions of the bedroom to whip male political defectors into conformity with 'self-interest,'" and headed angry mobs against unjust elections.[11] Moreover, emancipated black women were assertive and determined as they struggled to attain justice and economic security by demanding the fair payment of wages (e.g., in 1866, the black washerwomen in Jackson,

Mississippi, collectively agreed to charge a standard rate for their work), even if such resulted in physical violence against them.[12] Black professional women increased their efforts in the service of black people as educators and reformers. Some traveled to the South to work among the freedpersons; others remained in the North as advocates and activists. The aim of the first group was to ameliorate social and economic conditions that were undermining emancipation in the South and that of the second group was to confront the possible negative effect of the failure of such upon the lives of all black people across the country.

Of course, all of these political, economic, educational, and social strides were being undertaken against continuing sexual exploitation and devaluation of black womanhood in both the South and North. The social myths of black womanhood from slavery, Jezebel and Mammy, were being transformed by the times. Two new myths came to the fore and would persist into the twentieth century: "the bad black woman" and "the black rapist."[13] These were the necessary prongs in the social control of black people who now had the possibility of concerted national action against racial discrimination as a legally free people. The alleged immorality of black women coupled with the supposed bestiality of black men were complementary elements undergirding the continuing racial ideology of the black child/savage.

Overall, emancipation was not a boon for the majority of black women:

> *only an infinitesimal number of Black women had managed to escape from the fields, from the kitchen or from the washroom. According to the 1890 census, there were 2.7 million Black girls and women over the age of ten. More than a million of them worked for wages: 38.7 percent in agriculture; 30.8 percent in household domestic service; 15.6 percent in laundry work; and a negligible 2.8 percent in manufacturing.*[14]

Thus, given the debilitating social and economic realities in spite of legal emancipation, it is not surprising that black women made up a large percentage of the migration to town and cities in the South and North which culminated in the urbanization of the black population by the late nineteenth and early twentieth centuries. The following reasons for and consequences of black women's migration are further critical earmarks which distinguish their experience.[15]

First, single mothers with children and widows were particularly prominent among migrants in the South because of the difficulty of maintaining an economically viable agrarian livelihood for the support of a family. In fact, "the predominance of the female element [was] perhaps the most striking phenomenon of the urban Negro population."[16] There were high percentages of female-headed families and women in the paid labor force (50 to 70 percent of all adult black females were gainfully employed at least part-time in large southern cities at the turn of the century). Three times as many black as white women listed an occupation from 1870–1880—two-thirds of single black women and one-third of single white women, 31 percent of married black women and 4 percent of married white women reported jobs. Also, while white southern women who migrated into southern towns and cities worked in textile and tobacco factories, the majority of black women were employed in white households or other service occupations (e.g., nurses, cooks, washerwomen chambermaids, and seamstresses).[17]

Second, the prospect of better wages in industrial cities of the North made them attractive to southern black women who as farm laborers and urban domestics were paid $.75 a day and $1.50 to $3.00 a week, respectively. At least the northern cities held out the possibility of earning as much as $3 or $4 a day in factories and $2.50 a day for domestic work. However, because of the higher cost of living in the North the difference in wages was neutralized, and black women frequently found that their standard of living was actually lowered. Also, young illiterate black girls were often lured northward by labor agents who had them sign contracts that required that they pay the cost of the trip as well as a placement fee; many times these agents promised the girls domestic service when they were actually recruiting them for brothels.[18]

These conditions surrounding black female migration affected class tensions within the black community and fed white society's general negative assessment of Blacks against white middle-class standards for womanhood, family life, and economic progress. Since the black female migrants primarily swelled the class of unskilled laborers, their presence contributed further to the antagonism between migrants and black residents of the cities. Because black women worked in large numbers outside of the home and given the types of work they did, black womanhood continued to be devalued.

In summary, these sociohistorical and economic features constituted the particular contours of black women's experience within the evolution of black social stratification. It is not the contention here that black women stood outside of the evolution of social stratification and its dilemma; rather, it is that gender differentiated how black women experienced, understood, and responded to such. Black women found that their gender leveled out their experiences across class lines, and, consequently, their race-gender-class consciousness and ideologies for racial advancement reflected this fact of their existence. It is thus the negative interaction of gender with race and class within the lives of black women, regardless of whether they were slaves, free laborers, or professional women that shaped "black women's perspective" on the dilemma. Their race-gender-class consciousness brought forth public responses that challenged both the racist and classist norms for womanhood and black life overall.

### Race-Gender-Class Consciousness of Black Women

The public responses of black women were articulated as they participated in religion, education, and social reform. These responses denoted ethical reflection and moral agency deriving from a combination of religious faith and race-gender-class consciousness. As Marilyn Richardson wrote, "Religious faith gave [black] women strength, courage, comfort, and above all, vision—a vision that was at once creative, intellectual, and pragmatic."[19]

This faith produced a socioreligious ethical perspective that undergirded black women's social activism throughout slavery, emancipation, and urbanization. Black women from diverse walks of life—wealthy, educated, free women; poor, minimally or uneducated bondwomen or freewomen; women within reform movements, such as the temperance and club movements; preachers and evangelists within or outside the confines of the organized church—all articulated this perspective that undergirded their moral agency. Black women often acknowledged the call of God to challenge evils within society, drew connections between their religious sensibilities and the meaning of social justice, and offered rigorous analyses of both the external and internal dimensions of black oppression. Their ethical perspective yielded critical and sometimes constructive insights with respect to society, in general, and the black community, in particular. Some representative voices of the nineteenth and early twentieth centuries illustrate this perspective.

Isabella Baumfree [Sojourner Truth] (ca. 1797–1883), a former slave who became a famous antislavery lecturer and woman's rights advocate, understood her mission and message in the following way:

> *The Lord has made me a sign unto this nation, an' I go round a' testifyin', an' showin' their sins agin my people. My name was Isabella; but when I left the house of bondage, I left everything behind. I wa'n't goin' to keep nothin' of Egypt on me, an' so I went to the Lord an' asked him to give me a new name. An the Lord gave me Sojourner, because I was to travel up an' down the land, showin' the people their sins, an' bein' a sign unto them. Afterward I told the Lord I wanted another name, 'cause everybody else had two names; and the Lord gave me Truth, because I was to declare the Truth to the people.*
>
> *. . . I journeys round to campmeetin's, an' wherever folks is, an' I sets up my banner, an' then I sings, an' then folks always come up round me, an' then I preaches to 'em. I tells 'em about Jesus, an' I tells 'em about the sins of this people.*[20]

Sojourner Truth's words point to the relationship between religious faith and social criticism at the heart of black women's socioreligious ethical perspective.

In a similar vein, Maria W. Stewart (1803–1879), an impoverished free northeastern black woman who is believed to be the first American-born woman to lecture before a "promiscuous" (i.e., composed of men and women) audience, wrote this critique of the United States in her book *Religion and the Pure Principles of Morality, The Sure Foundation on Which We Must Build*:

> *Oh, America, America, foul and indelible is thy stain! Dark and dismal is the cloud that hangs over thee, for thy cruel wrongs*

*and injuries to the fallen sons of Africa. The blood of her murdered
ones cries to heaven for vengeance against thee. Thou art almost
become drunken with the blood of her slain; thou hast enriched
thyself through her toils and labors; and now thou refuseth to
make even a small return. And thou hast caused the daughters of
Africa to commit whoredoms and fornications; but upon thee be
their curse.*[21]

Significantly, one finds in Maria Stewart's words an example of
an analysis of the complexity of black oppression. It is the type of
criticism of the external dimension of black oppression that arises
out of black women's race-gender-class consciousness. She recognized the economic roots of racist injustice to Blacks in the refusal
of America to make reparation and acknowledged the form of
gender oppression perpetrated against black women. Stewart
knew that black oppression was clearly not limited to racist domination but was bound up with gender and economic exploitation.

Furthermore, the race-gender-class consciousness of Dr. Anna
Julia Cooper (1858–1964), who was born a slave in North Carolina
and became an educator and principal in the Washington, D.C.,
public schools, led her to make these penetrating remarks in an
address, "The Ethics of the Negro Question" (1902):

*Professing a religion of sublime altruism, a political faith in the
inalienable rights of man as man, these jugglers with reason and
conscience were at the same moment stealing heathen from their
far away homes, forcing them with lash and gun to unrequited
toil, making it a penal offense to teach them to read the Word of
God,—nay, more, were even begetting and breeding mongrels of
their own flesh among these helpless creatures and pocketing the
guilty increase, the price of their own blood in unholy dollars and
cents. Accursed hunger for gold!*

*. . . [It] is our hope today that the petrifying spirit of commer-
cialism which grows so impatient at the Negro question or any
other questions calculated to weaken the money getting nerve by
pulling at the heart and the conscience may still find a worthy
protagonist in the reawakened ethical sense of the nation which
can take no step backward and which must eventually settle, and*

*settle right this and every question involving the nation's honor and integrity.*[22]

Most important, Cooper here denounces the United States' betrayal of its religious, political, and ethical ideals in pursuit of financial gain because such has impaired the "ethical sense of the nation." Hers is an ardent commentary on the subversion of justice and morality by economic interests as the grounding for black oppression.

One finds complementary sentiments in the remarks by an anonymous black woman writing to *The Independent* (September 18, 1902):

> *The Southerner boasts that he is our friend; he educates our children, he pays us for work and is most noble and generous to us. Did not the Negro by his labor for over three hundred years help to educate the white man's children? Is thirty equal to three hundred? Does a white man deserve praise for paying a black man for his work?*
>
> *The Southerner also claims that the Negro gets justice. Not long ago a Negro man was cursed and struck in the face by an electric car conductor. The Negro knocked the conductor down and although it was clearly proven in a court of "justice" that the conductor was in the wrong the Negro had to pay a fine of $10. The judge told him "I fine you that much to teach you that you must respect white folks." The conductor was acquitted. "Most noble judge! A second Daniel!" This is the South's idea of justice. . . .*[23]

This woman candidly portrays the practical manifestations ("South's idea of justice") of the weak ethical nerve and perverted sense of justice that Cooper denounced. Her words reveal a clear understanding that freedom does not automatically entail either economic or legal justice.

Consequently, in addition to poignant analyses and critiques of the larger society, the race-gender-class consciousness and socioreligious ethical perspective of black women pushed them to criticize Blacks for (1) the ways in which their attitudes and behavior reflected oppressive ones of the larger society and (2) failing to

institute needed internal conditions within the black community
that were prerequisite for progress. These critiques of the internal
dimension of black oppression are powerfully directed at relations with the black church. For example, Jarena Lee (1783–?), an
evangelist who was denied ordination in the A.M.E. church,
made this argument in response to the educational elitism and
sexism of black clergy:

> *O how careful ought we to be, lest through our by-laws of
> church government and discipline, we bring into disrepute even
> the word of life. For as unseemly as it may appear now-a-days for
> a woman to preach, it should be remembered that nothing is im-
> possible with God. And why should it be thought impossible, het-
> erodox, or improper for a woman to preach? Seeing the Savior
> died for the woman as well as for the man. . . . Is He not a whole
> Savior instead of a half one? As those who hold it wrong for a
> woman to preach would seem to make it appear.*
>
> *Did not Mary first preach the risen Savior, and is not the doc-
> trine of the resurrection the very climax of Christianity—hangs
> not all our hope on this, as argued by St. Paul? Then did not
> Mary, a woman, preach the Gospel? For she preached the resur-
> rection of the crucified Son of God.*
>
> *But some will say that Mary did not expound the Scripture,
> therefore she did not preach in the proper sense of the term. To this
> I reply, it may be that the word* preach *in those primitive times,
> did not mean exactly what it is now* made *to mean; perhaps it
> was a great deal more simple then, than it is now—if it were not,
> the unlearned fishermen could not have preached the Gospel at all,
> as they had no learning.*[24]

Julia Foote (1823–1900), daughter of former slaves and eventually ordained an elder in the A.M.E. Zion church, joined Lee as
she summed up gender oppression and the patriarchalism of
black clergy in this way: "There was no justice meted out to
women in those days. Even ministers of Christ did not feel that
women had any rights which they were bound to respect."[25] As an
interpreter of the social import of Foote's autobiography points
out, the language in this statement parodied the infamous language of the Dred Scott decision of 1857 in which Justice Taney

said that black Americans "had no rights which the white man was bound to respect." "Foote drew a parallel between political racism and ecclesiastical sexism, both sanctioned by an authority of power, not of justice."[26] The comments of both Lee and Foote suggested that the black community at times mimicked the worst in the larger society and that both elitism and sexism undergirded the exclusion of women from positions of power (the clergy) within the black community.

Maria Stewart, in an address delivered in 1832 to the Afric American Female Intelligence Society, chided Blacks for being "so unkind and so unfeeling" toward one another that they became in one sense their "greatest oppressors." She insisted that, even though Blacks were denied opportunity, they could become a "highly distinguished and intelligent people" by marshaling all their efforts. Stewart reminded black people to "promote and patronize each other," "possess the spirit of independence," "sue for [their] rights and privileges," and to "hearken unto the voice of the Lord, our God, and walk in his ways and ordinances, and become distinguished for our ease, elegance, and grace, combined with other virtues."[27]

In summation, she stated this:

> *But God has said, that Ethiopia shall stretch forth her hands unto him. True, but God uses means to bring about his purposes; and unless the rising generation manifest a different temper and disposition towards each other from what we have manifested, the generation following will never be an enlightened people.*[28]

Stewart challenged the black community to cultivate traits of character worthy of a liberated people that God had chosen for a greater destiny. She spoke of the need for black people to be economically self-determined, to seek legal restitution, and to be self-assured. Clearly, Stewart's faith pushed her to challenge the black community from theocentric standards—not racist, sexist, classist ones—for black life.

Likewise, Frances Ellen Watkins Harper (1825–1911), a free woman born in Baltimore and a seamstress, teacher, poet, and abolitionist lecturer throughout her life, wrote in an article in *The Anglo-African* (1859):

*We need what money cannot buy and what affluence is too beg-garly to purchase. Earnest, self-sacrificing souls that will stamp themselves not only on the present but the future. Let us not then defer all noble opportunities till we get rich. And here I am, not aiming to enlist a fanatical crusade against the desire for riches, but I do protest against chaining down the soul, with its Heaven endowed faculties and God given attributes to the one idea of get-ting money as stepping into power or even gaining our rights in common with others.*

*The respect that is only bought by gold is not worth much. It is no honor to shake hands politically with men who whip women and steal babies. If this government has no call for our services, no aim for our children, we have the greater need for them to build up a true manhood and womanhood for ourselves.*[29]

Harper admonished Blacks that money is necessary but not sufficient for the up-building of a people. Most important, Harper called the black community (women and men) to adopt an understanding of the relationship among money, self-worth, and self-determination as a people that countered the larger society's classist equation of financial worth and individual self-worth. She had a vision of community rather than individualism as the basis for racial progress.

From another angle, Nannie Helen Burroughs also commented on the problem of how black people should define their self-worth in an article "Not Color But Character" (1904):

*Many Negroes have colorphobia as badly as the white folk have Negrophobia. . . .*

*There is no denying it, Negroes have colorphobia. Some Negro men have it. Some Negro women have it. Whole families have it, and somebody tells me that some Negro churches have it. Saviour, keep us from those churches, please. Some social circles have it, and so the disease is spreading from men to women, from women to families, from families to churches, and from churches to social circles. The idea of Negroes setting up a color standard is preposterous.*[30]

Burroughs unapologetically condemned both black women and men for allowing color distinctions to stratify the community. She chided them for imposing whiteness as a normative physical and moral standard that distracted them from the greater task of community building. In so doing, Burroughs reminded black people that the larger systems of social and racial-ethnic stratification create a context for further stratification within the black community that diminished the character of black people.

These women's words reveal a consciousness and ethical perspective that illustrate the black women's grasp of the complexity of black oppression. On the one hand, black women were aware of an external dimension, and this produced an evaluation of the relation between economics and justice in society and an awareness of a connection between racial and gender oppression. On the other hand, they recognized an internal dimension, and this led to an acknowledgment of gender oppression in the black community, a call for self-help and economic self-determination, and a description of character traits for a self-determined people.

The black women's perspective on the dilemma of competitive individualism versus social responsibility was thus analytical and self-critical. Black women knew that black people had to analyze the context in which Blacks found themselves. Yet, they also insisted that black people not allow that context to define their responses, that they be self-critical and self-assured, rejecting racist, sexist, classist norms for black life and promoting community instead of competitive individualism.

Moreover, the women's race-gender-class consciousness alone did not constitute their perspective on the dilemma. For the most part, they criticized from a socioreligious ethical perspective that may be typified as a belief in both the justice of God and justice for Blacks as a command of God. This consciousness and ethical perspective, therefore, was the basis of their perspective on the dilemma and was foundational for a reform movement initiated by black women. That movement was a national black women's club movement.

## Context and Nature of the Club Movement

The context in which a national black women's club movement emerged was earmarked by the growth of women's organizations in the nineteenth century generally.

> *The development of the Woman's Christian Temperance Union and the success of the Grange among rural women during the last quarter of the nineteenth century heralded an era in which American women joined together to form a multitude of clubs, leagues, societies, and associations. Between 1890 and 1920, this "associating" tendency reached fulfillment as millions of women organized into thousands of separate groups.*[31]

Although the types of groups within the club movement were diverse (literary societies, social clubs, professional clubs, prayer circles, Dorcas societies), most interpreters of the late nineteenth-century women's club movement characterize it principally as nonsectarian and autonomous (not an auxiliary of male organizations) and suggest that this critically distinguishes it from precedent groups in the earlier part of the century.[32] This characterization applies to the black women's club movement[33] and is important for understanding the thought and work of the movement which will be examined later.

When black women organized the National Association of Colored Women (NACW) by merging the National Federation of Afro-American Women and the League of Colored Women in 1896, they became a *socioreligious* movement against race, gender, and class oppression while working for the advancement of all black people. On the one hand, the black women's club movement was a *social* movement; it was the means through which black women created a "milieu" wherein they could question "accepted relations of power and the ideological underpinnings of those relations" and develop "programs, agendas, and justifications" for the society they sought to reform through ideas that derived from their unique race-gender-class consciousness.[34]

As a social movement, NACW was both a sponsor of national programs and "the first cohesive national network of black women." It was a social reform organization whose very structure constituted support networks. "The structure of the organization facilitated communication: local clubs at the base, then state federations, regional federations, and at the top the national body. Information and influence flowed freely from bottom to top as well as in the reverse direction."[35] Eventually, the NACW would affiliate with organizations in Canada, Liberia, and Madagascar and with the National Council of Women and the International Council of Women, help form the International Council of Women of the Darker Races, and participate in the national suffrage and temperance movements.[36]

On the other hand, the black women's club movement was a *religious* movement with respect to the training for leadership obtained in and continuing congenial ties with the church (i.e., some local member clubs were, in fact, church groups). Fannie Barrier Williams, a club woman and journalist of the period, wrote in 1900:

> *The training which first enabled colored women to organize and successfully carry on club work was originally obtained in church work. . . . . The churches have been sustained, enlarged and beautified principally through the organized efforts of their women members. The meaning of unity of effort for the common good, the development of social sympathies grew into women's consciousness through the privileges of church work.*[37]

The religious ethical sense ("unity of effort for the common good"), which Williams described black women as having developed through church work, and the ability of church groups to participate in a nonsectarian reform movement are significant points I wish to emphasize in this characterization of the club movement as *socioreligious.*

The club movement embodied the black women's existence as a distinct sociohistorical group, and a comparative look at a few aspects of the black and white women's club movements is instructive with regard to this point. That is, although the national black women's club movement developed during the time of (between 1892 and 1894) and even parallel to the white women's club movement, the motivations, intents, and aims of the two movements were dissimilar because of the different sociohistorical and economic bases. This discussion does not ignore that racism was a critical factor inhibiting black women's participation in the white women's club movement. However, the formation of a separate black women's club movement was more than a defensive reaction because of racist exclusion; it was an act of self-determination to address the particular concerns of black women and all black people.

The white women's club movement promoted activism outside the home in terms of the morally superior values which they believed that women could transmit to society.[38] A concept of "virtuous womanhood" and an "ideology of educated motherhood" served as the bases for their social reform activism. From the perspective of "virtuous womanhood," the person more than the system was in need of reform. Social problems were perceived as moral problems, and voluntary social reform efforts (e.g., temperance unions, mission societies, aid associations, women's clubs) were designed to eliminate corruption. From the perspective of an "ideology of educated motherhood," an emphasis was placed on the needs of the child and the need to train women for the tasks of motherhood. It brought together the duties of motherhood and the value of a college education. Social problems were recognized as deriving from external conditions such as industrialization, urbanization, and immigration; social reform programs were preventive programs.[39]

The black women's club movement also maintained a concept of "virtuous womanhood" and an "ideology of educated motherhood." But, because black women as a group confronted a white supremacist society which placed them outside of the social and moral community they sought to reform, their club work had to be intrinsically political and economic as well as ethical. In other words, the black club women's interpretation of the concept and ideology of womanhood was construed by their experience as women who were treated as anomalies in the society from which they were seeking justice.

The black women's cognizance of being anomalies to society's ideals of womanhood is particularly borne out when one considers that the first national conference of black women (1895) was convened partly in response to a public assault upon black womanhood. Seeking to discredit Ida B. Wells (a black journalist and the leading spokesperson against lynching at the time), a white male Missouri editor wrote a letter to Florence Balgarnie (a British suffragist and reformer who had invited Wells to conduct her antilynching campaign abroad) indicting all black women as "natural thieves, liars and prostitutes." Balgarnie forwarded the

letter to Josephine St. Pierre Ruffin, an organizer of one of the first
black women's clubs, The Woman's Era Club of Boston. With this
letter in hand, Mrs. Ruffin issued a call for a national meeting of
black women through *The Woman's Era*. The following are excerpts from that call and a letter that accompanied it.

> *The coming together of our women from all over the country for*
> *consultation, for conference, for the personal exchange of greeting,*
> *which means so much in the way of encouragement and inspira-*
> *tion, has been a burning desire in the breasts of the colored women*
> *in every section of the United States. . . .*
>
> *Although this matter of a convention has been talked over for*
> *some time, the subject has been precipitated by a letter to England,*
> *written by a southern editor, and reflecting upon the moral char-*
> *acter of all colored women; this letter is too indecent for publica-*
> *tion, but a copy of it is sent with this call to all the women's bodies*
> *throughout the country. Read this document carefully and use*
> *discriminately and* decide if it be not time for us to stand be-
> fore the world and declare ourselves and our principles.
>
> *The time is short, but everything is ripe; and remember, earnest*
> *women can do anything. . . . Although we do not hope that this*
> *our first conference will in all respects meet our ideal, yet* we
> trust that it will be the beginning of a movement for creat-
> ing a community of interest among all earnest women who
> love purity and demand justice.
>
> *The letter of Mr. Jacks which is also enclosed is only used* to
> show how pressing is the need of our banding together if
> only for our protection; *this is only one of the many matters*
> *upon which we need to confer. . . .*
>
> *This invitation is extended to all colored women of America,*
> *members of any society or not.*[40]

Ruffin's call made note that the experience of black women generated its own ethics ("declare ourselves and our principles").
The aim of the meeting was clearly to initiate a social justice
movement led by and for all black women.

Although both the black and the white women's club movements were led primarily by middle-class women,[41] there are
clear differences. For white women, their middle-class status led

them most often to concern themselves with issues such as property rights and the exclusion of women from occupations for
which their education had prepared them; issues of limited relevance to poor and working-class women's lives. However, for
black women, the fact that their middle class status was attained
in spite of and maintained under conditions of racist caste-class
oppression led them to view issues more systemically.[42] Significantly, unlike their white counterparts, the leaders of the black
women's club movement "frequently successfully bridged the
class barrier and concerned themselves with issues of importance
to poor women, working mothers, and tenant farm wives."[43]

As a group, the black club movement's leaders manifested a
less classist attitude toward the masses of black people than did
some black elite and the society in general. This interpretation
does not overlook the elitism that black club leaders could exemplify. However, the critical difference was that the elitism of the
black women's clubs emphasized social reform priorities that included upward social and economic mobility for everyone,
whereas the classist elitism of white club women showed little
concern for needs and aspirations of poorer classes.[44]

The black club women's experience had taught them that creating the "opportunity and environment for all Black women"[45] was
critical. They also recognized the impact of institutional classism
upon the lives of black people. "Almost every black women's
club, regardless of who founded it or the ostensible reason for its
establishment, focused to some extent on alleviating one or more
of the many social problems afflicting an increasingly urban, impoverished, politically powerless, and segregated black population."[46] In sum, the black club women understood the work of
their movement thus: "The club movement among colored
women reaches into the sub-social condition of the entire race."[47]

With this discussion of the context and nature of the club
movement in mind, it can be asserted that the National Association of Colored Women (NACW) was a socioreligious movement
that created a milieu in which black women questioned the ideological underpinnings of racist, sexist, and classist oppression in
society. It is now feasible to examine the club women's thought
and work—their justifications and programs for the society they
wanted to create.

## Representative Thought and Work of the Club Movement

The key relationship to be explicated here is the one between the black club women's race-gender-class consciousness and their programs to alleviate race, gender, and class oppression. A place to begin this explication is with the name: the National Association of Colored Women. This is important because (as stated in chapter 3) the choice of a name to designate the race signaled class biases. In the 1890s when the national organization originated, the terms "Afro-American" and "Negro" were most often used by the protest/nationalist and accommodative/integrationist camps, respectively. What does it mean that this organization chose the term "colored" rather than Afro-American or Negro?

As mentioned above, the NACW was the result of the union of the Federation of Afro-American Women and the Colored Women's League. During the committee meeting on union there was considerable debate as to a name for the new organization. This debate reflected the tension between conservative and radical thinkers within the movement that would be successfully mediated. Those who favored "colored" in the name argued that since "the race was known in the census as colored people," this was an appropriate designation. Those proposing "Afro-American" argued that an African heritage and birth in America "entitled" them to the name "Afro-American" just as Anglo-Americans were entitled to so designate themselves.[48] It is not clear from the minutes exactly how this dispute was resolved and consensus reached. However, given that Mary Church Terrell chaired the joint committee and was elected by them to be the first president of the consolidated organization, it seems reasonable to infer that her understanding of the term "colored" became the operational definition. Terrell felt that the variety of skin color and varied origins of black people was best represented by the term "colored."[49]

The use of the term "colored" may thus be interpreted as an attempt to acknowledge the diversity within the black community rather than a throwback to an earlier era when "colored" signified denial of both an African heritage and/or the need for separate black institutions. The club women had a heightened race consciousness, affirming the particular needs of black women, men, and children and emphasizing programmatically race history education. Perhaps, the name for the organization further signified that the group was conscious of an inherent tension between the diversity of and the need for unity within the black community.

Moreover, the address of Josephine St. Pierre Ruffin at the first national conference of black women (1895) suggested a guiding ethical premise for the programs that the NACW would decide to undertake in 1896. She said that black women needed to gather in order to nurture a sense of unity premised upon mutual inspiration and encouragement. Her remarks conclude:

> *Our woman's movement is woman's movement in that it is led and directed by women for the good of women and men, for the benefit of all humanity, which is more than any one branch or section of it. We want, we ask the active interest of our men, and, too, we are not drawing the color line; we are women, American women, as intensely interested in all that pertains to us as such as all other American women; we are not alienating or withdrawing, we are only coming to the front, willing to join any others in the same work and cordially inviting and welcoming any others to join us.*
>
> *If there is any one thing I would especially enjoin upon this conference it is union and earnestness. . . . If any differences arise let them be quickly settled, with the feeling that we are all workers to the same end, to elevate and dignify colored American womanhood.*[50]

The ethical premise of Ruffin's words is that of an intrinsic connection between the particular and the universal; this connection meant that club women believed that their work on behalf of black women (the particular) was related to the greater good of society (the universal). It was reiterated throughout Ruffin's address as she summoned the women as *colored* women to unite within the context of a *woman's movement* which was *"for the benefit of all humanity."* Likewise, the guiding programmatic emphases were specific concerns of black women such as social, moral, and economic training for the children and youth as well as the broader issues of the day, such as temperance, morality, higher education, hygienic, and domestic questions.

By the time that 61 delegates met for the NACW's first convention in September, 1897, at Howard Chapel Congregational Church in Nashville, Tennessee, that which Ruffin had projected in 1895 had taken root. At that meeting, the constitution was adopted; the Preamble and Article II (dealing with NACW's objective) from it read:

### *Preamble*

*We, the Colored Women of the United States of America, feeling the need of united and systematic effort, and hoping to furnish evidence of the moral, mental, and material progress made by people of color through the efforts of our women, do hereby unite in a national association of colored women.*

### *Article II*
### *Object*

*The object of this Association shall be by the help of God to secure harmony of action and cooperation among all women in raising to the highest plane, home, moral and civil life.*[51]

Mary Church Terrell, the first president of the association, commented upon the name and purpose of the organization in her address:

*We call ourselves an "Association" to signify that we have joined hands one with another to work together in a common cause; to proclaim to the world that the women of our race have become partners in the great firm of progress and reform.*

*We denominate ourselves "Colored," not because we are narrow, and wish to lay special emphasis upon the color of the skin, for which no one is responsible, which of itself is a proof neither of an individual's virtue nor of his vice, which is a stamp neither of one's intelligence nor of his ignorance, but we refer to the fact that this is an Association of Colored Women, because our peculiar status in this country at the present time seems to demand that we stand by ourselves in the special work for which we have been organized. For this reason and for no other it was thought best to invite the attention of the world to the fact that colored women feel their responsibility as a unit and together have clasped hands to assume it.*[52]

Terrell's words portrayed the NACW's vision of itself as an organization that claimed the sociohistoric particularity of black women as the basis and *raison d'etre* for its existence and work. The race-gender-class consciousness expressed by Terrell might be described as an unapologetic acknowledgment of black women's reality within the context of black oppression.

This consciousness was quite alive in the 61 delegates from 59 member clubs (42 of which were located in urban areas) at that first convention.[53] Also, the reports of the clubs at this convention evidence ways in which the association was a socioreligious movement working for the alleviation of race-gender-class oppression from the premise that the particular and the universal are intrinsically connected. The following are excerpts from reports received at that convention.[54]

### Women's League of Wilmington, Del.

. . . *Our League was organized Mar. 9, 1897 with a number of very earnest women. We now no. 83. Our object in organization was to establish an Industrial School, for our girls. We feel the need of training the hand, as well as the Head and esspecial [sic] to impress upon our girls that Labor is Honorable. We therefore are trying to make it possible for them to learn the science of labor. And if it is cooking, washing, or ironing, do it in that manner that no one else can do it any better . . . not trying to do too many things but to help fallen women in our community in a way that may be felt.*

### The Phillis [sic] Wheatley Club of New Orleans

*The Phillis Wheatley Club of New Orleans beg leave to submit to you this their annual report. The work begun by the club has progressed; each and every member taking an active interest in furthering the object for which the club was organized viz.: the uplifting of our people.*

*The one great object toward which our combined efforts were extended was the establishment of a Sanitorium and Training School for Nurses. We needed a Sanitorium where the suffering ones of our people could receive proper attention both as pay and as charity patients since colored patients are not received in the pay wards of our other hospitals. We also needed a place where our young medical students could receive that practice, so essential to every doctor's success. They are debarred this privilege in the other hospitals even in the colored wards. The Training School for Nurses was opened in order to introduce our young women into a lucrative field of labor. We recognized the necessity of the training since all trades and professions are now calling for trained hands.*

### *The Phyllis Wheatley Women's League of Chicago*
*. . . We have made a special study of the history of the Negro Race in America feeling that many of our women are ignorant of the grand achievements of their own race, and we know that we have been greatly benefitted. . . . The Philanthropic section worked hard last winter in caring for the sick and needy, one family became the especial care of the Club &, was supplied with food, fuel and clothing.*

From these reports to the first biennial convention, outlines of the black club women's interpretation of the racial ideology of self-help and racial solidarity for racial advancement emerge. Out of their race-gender-class consciousness, black club women sought to implement programs that would promote cultural revitalization as well as social rehabilitation. They knew that racial advancement had to rest upon a dynamic interplay between critical self-understanding of and socioeconomic response to the realities of the race's condition in society. Such is the real meaning behind the Phyllis Wheatley Women's League of Chicago's special study of the history of the race in the U.S., the Women's League of Wilmington's industrial school, and the Phillis Wheatley Club of New Orleans's sanitorium and training school for nurses. The programs were responsive to the needs (for self-knowledge and for job training and health services) of black people and were not merely a defensive reaction to race and class oppression.

Most important, local club programs embodied and enacted what club leaders were writing about the black woman's condition within the black community and in the larger society. For example, when the Women's League of Wilmington, Delaware, decided to establish an industrial school for black girls, they were not merely adopting the theory of social rehabilitation associated with Booker T. Washington or capitulating to an oppressive classist view of society that maintains the necessity of menial laboring classes. Instead, they had an understanding of the situation as expressed by Nannie Helen Burroughs (head of the Young Women's Work Department of NACW, 1910–1912) when she wrote about "the domestic problem." Burroughs pointed out the relationship between just compensation for domestic labor and being adequately trained and stressed to all classes of black people the respectability of domestic work:

> *Our women have worked as best they could without making any improvements and thus developing the service into a profession, and in that way make the calling more desirable from a standpoint of being lifted from a mere drudgery, as well as from the standpoint of compensation received. . . .*
>
> *Our "high-toned" notions as to the kind of positions educated people ought to fill have caused many women who can not get anything to do after they come out of school to loaf rather than work for an honest living, declaring to themselves and acting it before others, that they were not educated to live among pots and pans. None of us may been educated for that purpose, but educated women without work and the wherewith to support themselves and who have declared in their souls that they will not stoop to toil are not worth an ounce more to the race than ignorant women who have made the same declarations. Educated loafers will bear as much watching as ignorant ones. . . . What matters is if our women, by honest toil, make their way from the kitchen to places of respect and trust in the walks of life? . . . It is not the depth from which we come, but the heights to which we soar.*[55]

A club that established an industrial school to train women in the "science of [domestic] labor" did so because it recognized society's growing demand for skilled labor and to ensure that black women were competitive in the job market, to provide an educational means for further progress for a significant part of the black population, and to counter elitist attitudes within the black community that denigrated domestic service. Although the work of clubs in this regard was not radical in the sense of a socialist critique of a capitalist society's labor structure, the work had at least a latent liberative intent considering the emphasis on educating (not merely training) people to just compensation and their means for advancement. Indeed, Burroughs's remarks imply that club women believed that an educated labor force was important to both the economic and social advancement of black people.

The club women's analysis of labor issues and work on behalf of the black labor force continued throughout the late nineteenth and into the early twentieth century. For example, the Chicago Woman's Club held a conference on "Women in Modern Industrialism" in April, 1904. The speakers were described as having "urged a more inclusive sympathy and a more courageous stand for what is just and true in economic affairs." The conference succeeded in bringing to the fore the connection between race oppression and class oppression in the United States:

> *the fact is that the spirit of injustice that we [black people] contend against is the same spirit of injustice that millions of white men, women, and children are everywhere struggling against in the form of oppressive hours of labor, inadequate wages, unsanitary conditions of employment and the many inequalities that are crystallized into law and custom.*[56]

Conferences were not the only means for continued attention to economic issues. Some clubs engaged in boycotting efforts of businesses, such as "the National Biscuit Company which had suddenly discharged its thousands of colored employees."[57] Still others took up the utilitarian work of providing homes for wage-earning girls in the cities (e.g., the Afro-American Woman's Industrial Club of Jersey City, which purchased a house and employed a housekeeper because of their "desire to be able to care for all or at least a large part of the girls and women who come to our city from various parts of the country seeking employment and often, unfortunately, falling into bad hands").[58]

At the 1897 NACW convention, resolutions were adopted suggesting that the clubs petition state legislatures to repeal the separate railway-car laws; petition the Tennessee Industrial School to admit black boys; endorse the establishment of a John Brown Industrial School, the Douglass Memorial Monument, homes for the infirm and elderly, and reformatories for delinquents; and oppose juvenile secret societies, crime, the liquor traffic, and lynching.[59] As these resolutions suggest, NACW was clearly aware of the issues of the day and made such their priorities.

At the second convention (August 14–16, 1899), 144 delegates representing 46 clubs in 16 states met in Chicago to report further progress in club work aimed at alleviating the oppression of black women as well as the race and to discuss again the pressing social and economic issues of the day. An editorial from the *Chicago Daily News*, August 16, 1899, commented:

> *Of all the conventions that have met in the country this summer there is none that has taken hold of the business in hand with more good sense and judgment than the National Association of Colored Women, now assembled in this city. The subjects brought up, the manner of their treatment and the decisions reached exhibit wide and appreciative knowledge of conditions confronting the colored people.*[60]

The presidential address by Mary Church Terrell was entitled "The Progress of Colored Women." Terrell spoke forthrightly about depravity experienced by black women during slavery; cited the ways in which colored women had shown responsibility ("shirking responsibility has never been a fault with which colored women might be truthfully charged") by obtaining education, becoming teachers, agitating against unjust laws, and purifying the home; and admonished her white sisters that they had a critical task to raise children who "respect the lofty principles of justice and humanity upon which this government was founded and of which their consciences approve" if they did not wish to be judged harshly by God.[61]

Terrell spoke about the history of brutalization of black women against the backdrop of the ideologies of virtuous womanhood and educated motherhood as well as the black women's sense of God's justice. On the one hand, Terrell's remarks contrasted the experience of systemic racist gender oppression of black women to the professed ideal of virtuous womanhood ("so fatal the laws, so pernicious the customs").[62] On the other, she appealed to white mothers "to observe and teach their children to respect the lofty principles of justice and humanity" and to empathize with colored mothers' hopes for their children's future. In appealing to the ideology of educated motherhood, she made that ideology foundational to moral and social reform for racial justice contingent upon the training of the next generation by women.

This address was published and the proceeds from its sale were donated to a fund for the support of kindergartens, "the first department organized by the National Association." The sale of this pamphlet meant "that delegates were not only deciding on kindergartens [as a area of club work] but developing immediately a support for them."[63] As support for kindergartens suggests, by the 1899 convention and through the 1920s, the NACW's agenda clearly derived from a concept of virtuous womanhood and ideology of educated motherhood from the black woman's perspective. Among the work cited as most critical were the establishment of kindergartens, day nurseries, and mothers' clubs. Such work was critical because of their belief that this was essential to race elevation. What differentiates this belief on the part of black women from the white women's sense that women's virtues were needed for a higher moral standard in society is the fact that black women admonished both women and men to this responsibility in light of the impact of the slavery past upon the institution of the black family. "[B]ut none the less do we need for the creation of an inspired home life, of grand human life, of sublime national life, a conscious and ideal fatherhood."[64]

Southern clubs were especially active in this work since there were few kindergartens in the public schools for black children. The motivating factors for and aims of the work are expressed well in an article by Mrs. A. H. Hunton in which she noted that this endeavor was not solely a response to the failure of society to provide the service and as a means for moral training for children about their relationship to others and to God but also that it was a recognition of the working mothers' needs and a means for uplifting the masses.[65]

Kindergarten programs and all other work of the club movement arose from the black women's race-gender-class consciousness and socioreligious ethical perspective. To what degree the thought and work of the black women's club movement offer a paradigm for a mediating ethic for black liberation is addressed in the next chapter.

# 5

# What Do Nineteenth-Century Reformers Have to Say to Twentieth-Century Liberationists?

The aim of this book has been to discern socioreligious meaning for intragroup social responsibility that can serve as the basis of a mediating ethic for black liberation. The first two of the three tasks of ethical analysis to achieve that aim have been undertaken: the descriptive—an interpretation of the ethical dilemma deriving from social stratification in the black community, i.e., competitive individualism versus intragroup social responsibility (chapter 2), along with a sociohistorical description of the origin and evolution of that stratification and its dilemma (chapter 3) and (2) the critical—an examination of the response of Blacks themselves to the dilemma, i.e., the race-class consciousness of black men (chapter 3), race-gender-class consciousness of black women and the work of the black women's club movement (chapter 4). It is now appropriate to initiate the normative task.

My use of "mediating" differs somewhat from a denotative understanding that mediation aims at integration, compromise, or reconciliation. Here mediating refers more to the *process* of acknowledging seemingly diametrically opposing positions and *creating* a response that in effect interposes and communicates *between* the opposing sides. This interposition and communication between the opposing sides may be best understood as *living in tension with* rather than as aiming at an end result of integration, compromise, or reconciliation of such. Integration, compromise, or reconciliation may be an outcome but *mediating as process* has occurred whether or not mediation as an end does. The purpose of this chapter is to develop the paradigm for a mediating ethic embodied in the club movement. Finally, elements for a mediating ethic will be ascertained by bringing the club women's understanding of socioreligious ethical responsibility, the mainstream ethical tradition of responsibility (specifically, the ethical thought of H. Richard Niebuhr), and black religious liberation and womanist thought into creative interaction.

## An Interpretation of the Club Movement

The black women's club movement was a socioreligious movement against race-gender-class oppression. It was a social movement because through it black women created a milieu in which they were empowered to reinterpret the dominate racial, sexual, and class ideologies which oppressed them as women, while providing programs that addressed the oppression of black people. It was a religious movement because (1) its leaders were largely trained within the church, (2) a continuing religious influence existed through the participation of church-affiliated clubs as well as the leadership's ties to the church, and (3) it institutionalized an ethical perspective which emanated from the faith of black women (i.e., a belief in both the justice of God and justice for Blacks as a command of God). Thus, the black women's club movement was a mediation of social and religious movements.

The uniqueness of the movement is expressed further by an account in the *Woman's Era* as the writer described the decision to form a woman's club in her city:

> The idea of organizing a social club, a literary club, a religious club, or some such club, by which we might diversify the ceaseless monotony o'erhanging us, has been, for a long time, agitating the minds of a few ladies in this city; but not until the meeting of the Woman's Congress, a few weeks since, did we fully realize the importance of such a move. Consequently, two or three of us held a consultation regarding the matter and decided to invite a few other ladies to meet in conference with us. On the day appointed for meeting seven or eight ladies joined us, and we readily agreed to take upon us the responsibility of a club—not a social club, for in that we could not help better the world; it meant, in substance, for a few of us to meet, have a pleasant time, and utterly ignore the rest of our sex who would like to join us. Not a literary club, for then, so to speak, there would be one woman out of every ten capable of sustaining or entering into the requirements of such an

*undertaking. Not a professional nor yet a denominational club, but a woman's club. The idea met with general approval and with those, though few in number, we organized the Woman's Mutual Improvement Club.*[1]

From this writer's words we can infer that the women themselves thought there was a distinctiveness about being women in association as a *woman's* club as opposed to social, literary, professional, or denominational clubs. Members were determined not to allow class, education, profession, or religious affiliation as criteria for exclusion from a movement that was intrinsically concerned about alleviating race-gender-class oppression.[2] Because the movement's aims were to meet the practical needs of all classes of women (e.g., mother's meetings for working mothers, industrial schools for girls, or training schools for nurses), these programs also addressed the underlying racist-sexist-classist assumptions of gender oppression experienced by black women (i.e., devaluation of black womanhood manifested by sexual exploitation, restricted occupational mobility, and limited access to education for professions and vocational training).

It is the argument here that the black women's club movement had from its inception an ethical premise regarding an intrinsic interrelation of the particular and the universal as constitutive of the common good. This premise was evident in the programming aims of the movement. Although these programs were designed to address the particular social, political, and economic needs of black women and/or all black people, they also promoted the common good of reform and justice in the larger society.

The motto of the NACW, "Lifting as We Climb," reflected the black women's understanding of the interconnectedness and interrelatedness of Blacks as a group. Historian Linda Perkins has identified the socioethical dimension of this understanding (on the part of black women individually and collectively throughout the nineteenth century) as one of racial obligation and duty intertwined with the ideal of racial uplift and elevation.[3] The religious dimension of this understanding, as discussed in chapter 4, may be understood as centered in the black women's belief in both the justice of God and justice for Blacks as a command of God. These dimensions coalesce, creating the ethical sense of *socioreligious* responsibility at the heart of the club movement.

Thus, as a movement operating from a sense of socioreligious responsibility, the black women's club movement offers a paradigm for response to the ethical dilemma of competitive individualism versus intragroup social responsibility within the black community. There are two primary reasons why this movement suggests an appropriate paradigm for responding to this ethical dilemma posed by social stratification. First, because the leaders of the movement were largely by reason of education, occupation, property, and/or wealth members of the old mulatto elite, the rising black elite, or the middle class of the 1890s, it is striking that their efforts exemplify a lessening of competitive class consciousness and an overcoming of false black consciousness (i.e., the lack of awareness of one another as interrelated) that might be expected when members of an upper socioeconomic strata decide to participate actively on behalf of and/or with members of lower strata.[4] It was not simply status anxiety that moved these women to action. They did not allow the privileges of their class to obstruct the greater good of group progress.[5] The success of the club women's efforts suggest that they consciously and concertedly mediated between the competing claims of their class interests and their race and gender group interests, between the competitive individualism of class and the communalism that their race and gender group status required.

Ideologically, this meant that club women advocated elements of both primary theories for racial advancement during the late nineteenth century—the theories of social rehabilitation and cultural revitalization described in chapter 3. On one hand, they affirmed the philosophy of self-help and racial solidarity as the basis for the economic and moral development of black people. On the other, they promoted the understanding of black history and experience as the context for the self-determination of black people. They mediated between the voices of Booker T. Washington and W. E. B. DuBois; they created their own response using strategies of both positions. The women understood that in order to respond to their situation they needed to be flexible, holding in tension the specific aims of racial elevation, amelioration of gender and class oppression, and comprehensive reform of society for the good of all citizens. At a time when other organizations were weakened by internal ideological battles between "radicals" and "conservatives" (to use Kelly Miller's terms), "the protest/accommodation debate never paralyzed the NACW as it did other Black organizations."[6]

Second, the black club women's ability to mediate between these competing claims derived from a certain logic, described in the Introduction as the "dialectics of black womanhood." This logic recognized internal and external dimensions of black oppression and that working to influence the internal conditions of black life had consequences for the external ones. Black club women exhibited intragroup social responsibility, a sense of racial obligation and duty, as the core value for "lifting as [they] climbed." Their logic was summarized by the words of Mary Church Terrell:

> *Carefully and conscientiously we shall study the questions which affect the race most deeply and directly. Against the convict lease system, the Jim Crow car laws, lynchings and all other barbarities which degrade us, we shall protest with such force of logic and intensity of soul that those who oppress us will either cease to disavow the inalienability and equality of human rights, or be ashamed to openly violate the very principles upon which this government was founded. By discharging our obligation to our children, by coming into the closest possible touch with the masses of our people, by studying the labor question as it affects the race, by establishing schools of domestic science, by setting a high moral standard and living up to it, by purifying the home, colored women will render their race a service whose value it is not in my power to estimate or express.*
>
> *. . . With courage born of success achieved in the past, with a keen sense of the responsibility which we must continue to assume we look forward to the future, large with promise and hope. Seeking no favors because of our color or patronage because of our needs, we knock at the bar of justice and ask for an equal chance.*[7]

It is evident in Terrell's words that the club women's "logic" called for programs that addressed criminal justice, child welfare, poverty, education, and labor, as well as the nurturance of moral integrity among Blacks themselves as points of contact between the external and internal dimensions of black oppression.

The black women's club movement is a paradigm for a mediating ethic because their thought and work arose out of a mediating posture whereby accommodative and aggressive social activism, religious radicalism for societal change, and progress for individual Blacks and Blacks as a group could be maintained. The club movement's process of mediating was exemplified in its ability to hold in creative tension their elitist desire for individual social advancement; their belief that a just God calls persons and communities to participate in creating a just society; their insistence that black people develop themselves economically and fight for economic justice in the society; their individual quests for self-actualization through education and professional opportunity; and their commitment to service of the entire community. How this paradigm can contribute to the content of a contemporary mediating ethic for black liberation is the subject to which I now turn.

### Elements for a Mediating Ethic of Black Liberation

Central to the club women's understanding of socioreligious ethical responsibility was a commitment to racial uplift and elevation (a teleological feature) and a sense of racial obligation and duty (a deontological feature). They understood socioreligious ethical responsibility as a unification of religious and social ethical concerns. On the teleological side, racial uplift and elevation was a matter of cultivating character traits that would contribute to the self-determination of the black community. On the deontological side, racial obligation and duty meant that ethical responsibility requires right acts—in this case, acts to uplift those who had less or were without educational, economic, and/or occupational advantages. Because the teleological and deontological were interactive in the black women's understanding, this suggests that their ethic was substantively and methodologically mediating—that is, it held in tension seemingly oppositional stances and generates avenues for creative response. Thus, the mediating ethic for which the ethic of the black women's club movement is a paradigm is, to use the language of H. Richard Niebuhr, an ethic of responsibility.[8]

The fact that the black women's socioreligious ethical understanding generated a socioreligious movement implies that they understood moral agency as a matter of what Niebuhr terms a "fitting" response. They were responding to the social emergency of worsening caste-class oppression of the black community. Their "fitting" response arose from an interpretation of worsening oppression in light of a slavery past. The club women's accountability for their actions as individuals participating in a social reform movement issued from their commitment to one another as black women as well as to the cause of the regeneration of the race and justice for Blacks in society.[9]

Moreover, there was a theocentric view of justice (the justice of God and justice for Blacks as a command of God) at the heart of the black club women's understanding of responsibility.[10] Their understanding of moral good and evil centered on God's justice motivated their work for the alleviation of black oppression from a self-critical stance. They criticized the black community when it used social stratification as the center of value instead of God's justice for the entire black community and society overall. From their perspective, God's justice was the core of universal responsibility; God's justice was the "universe" that qualified their interpretation of actions in "a life of responses to actions."[11]

Thus, the club women's responsible self knew itself in absolute dependence as a sociohistoric self, a self-in-community. This self responded contextually to and acted on behalf of all members of its community because of trust (faith) in God as the ultimate power which calls the sociohistoric self into existence—even as an act of God's justice. Black persons who are selves-in-community do not lose their individuality, only their competitive (defensive) individualism. Individuals are responsible selves insofar as their actions are responses out of faith in God's justice. Although persons as selves-in-community are individuals who must respond individually and personally to God, they know that it is through and within the sociohistoric community that they are selves judged, redeemed, and saved by God's justice while being called as moral agents to respond to acts of oppression in the universal context of God's justice.[12]

The conceptual center for a mediating ethic is thus relationality. Sociohistoric relationality is critical because it refers to two important features of this ethic. On the one hand, it signifies that this is an ethic of community, and members of the community are such because of sociohistoric realities as much as because they are members of some particular racial and/or gender group. On the other hand, this relationality stresses the need to assess critically sociohistoric realities as the basis for making strong ethical choices.[13]

The ethical choices will be strong because the basis for making ethical decisions includes particularity as a morally relevant factor which differentiates members of the group (such as class differences) while holding them accountable to one another. Moral responsibility based upon sociohistoric relationality is empirically grounded and moral obligations are experientially determined. Those who espouse sociohistoric relationality recognize that an apparent racial and/or gender connection between members of a group provides a necessary but insufficient condition for liberative interconnection. Sociohistoric relationality requires members of a community engaged in liberative moral agency to make "hard" ethical choices—that is, to determine priorities among the competing claims of diverse members of the group (e.g., class differences)—in light of the sociohistoric and/or socioeconomic context(s) in which members of the group are interacting.

In other words, the logic of the club women's ethic discussed above was a logic of interstructured oppression. This logic was required by the club women's socioreligious ethical sense of responsibility derived from their experience as a distinct sociohistoric group. It was a logic that had a contextual interactive, sociohistorical, socioethical basis. This logic insisted that racism, sexism, and classism are both parallel (have independent effects) and contextually interactive (provide contexts for each other) oppressive processes.

From this logic, one recognizes that the black community experiences racism, sexism, and classism in the larger context of the patriarchal, white racist, capitalist United States. But this logic also acknowledges that the black community can be the micro context in which these oppressive processes occur. A logic of interstructured oppression compels the black community to engage in comprehensive liberative activity—activity that requires that the macro and micro contexts or external and internal dimensions of black oppression be addressed through a mediating process whereby we live in the tension between the two contexts. This logic allows us to discern that the moral dilemma of competitive individualism versus intragroup social responsibility in the black community is intimately related to moral dilemmas inherent in the larger U.S. society—such as, economic expediency versus socioeconomic and moral justice, white supremacy versus racial inclusiveness, and complicity in versus responsibility for overcoming oppression.

Important to this logic was the vision of God's justice that allowed the club women to speak and act out of their sociohistoric particularity to the universal, to the greater good of community and social reform in the larger society. Their vision of God's justice meant that black liberation had to be guided by an ethical imperative to overcome oppressive processes for the sake of reunion in the black community and in the larger society. Such grappling toward reunion was a manifestation of God's justice.

The ethical imperative of reunion is critical for intragroup social responsibility. It emerges from the theocentric perspective of a God who liberates the oppressed, or, in the club women's perspective, from being called to participate in the justice of God. Consequently, ethical reflection and action begins with the premise that the oppressed are called to be co-participants with God in God's liberating activity within society and to make nonoppressive relationships both the means and end to liberation. Black persons are called to be responsible moral agents who work for just relations within, and justice for, the black community as a command of God, a command the meaning of which must be determined empirically in sociohistoric context. The vision of God's justice and the logic of interstructured oppression are thus the linchpins in an ethic that mediates religious, ethical, and social contextual meaning for black liberation.

The mediating ethic deriving from the club movement, therefore, resonates with the following understanding of liberation and responsibility in black religious liberation and womanist thought. Liberation is theologically and ethically understood as deriving from God in Christ's liberating activity on behalf of the poor and oppressed. It is to be a historical and political event and thus should be guided by norms and principles that are sociologically sound. The community of the oppressed is where these norms and principles are formulated, tested, and applied. Ethical responsibility includes obligation to the community, self-determination as a community, acceptance of moral choice as individuals, and values reorientation. In sum, liberation and responsibility are theologically and sociohistorically defined by and in the community of the oppressed.[14]

Significantly, the understanding of God's justice central for the club women's ethic is a primary point of contact with black liberation theological and womanist religious thought. The club women's belief in the justice of God and justice for Blacks as a command of God specifies the content of the theological assertion that God in Christ is liberator of the oppressed. Likewise, the centrality of the obligation to and self-determination of the black community, as well as the acceptance of moral choice and the need for values reorientation, were part of the club women's ethic. Yet, whereas black liberation theological thought (more than womanist religious thought) tends to stress the obligatory nature of responsibility, because the club women's ethic held the teleological and deontological in tension, there was also the sense of responsibility as a good to be manifested in both the character of individuals and the community. Although the club women's ethic originated from black people's reality, it was premised upon an understanding of God's justice as a universal context in which liberation occurs. The theocentric context of God's justice is the needed qualification for keeping an ethic for black liberation self-critical.

Finally, the ethic of the club women was a relational ethic of responsibility that made both black individuals and the community the subject of moral agency. Acts of oppression against or within the black community were thus interpreted from the universal perspective of God's justice. Moral agency and action on the part of oppressed Blacks were critiqued as well as continually subjected to reinterpretation from this perspective. To paraphrase Niebuhr from the club women's perspective, "God is acting out of God's justice in all actions upon you. So respond to all actions upon you as to respond to God's justice."

The club women's ethic was an ethic of responsibility premised upon God's justice; intragroup social responsibility was a core value in a mediating ethic for black liberation derived from the central concept of sociohistoric relationality. The ethic thus mediated between the universal and the particular within the struggle for black liberation. The elements for a mediating ethic of black liberation are thus: (1) an understanding that liberation of the oppressed is a part of God's justice that must be discerned within the oppressed community; (2) an assumption that intracommunal accountability is a necessary prerequisite for intercommunal reconciliation; and (3) processes of moral response that mediate between the tensions intrinsic in oppressive realities and the creative vision and praxis required for and generated by living with those tensions. How such a mediating ethic can help Blacks address specifically the ethical dilemma posed by social stratification in the black community is the concluding discussion of this chapter.

## Implications for Overcoming the Ethical Dilemma of Black Stratification

In chapter 2, social stratification within the community was described as a core ethical dilemma plaguing the efforts of Blacks working toward black liberation. This core dilemma is that of competitive individualism versus intragroup social responsibility. The dilemma has two primary manifestations: false black consciousness (lack of awareness of one another as related selves, as selves-in-community) and "sympathy without empathy" (unwillingness of upper-class and middle-class Blacks to participate actually with or on behalf of lower-class Blacks to effect mutual, comprehensive liberation).

Other writers have described the dilemma in terms of the strains created by black stratification. This simply recognizes that at this point in history in the United States, social mobility is considerably more real for some Blacks than others. This in turn means that the efforts of the civil rights movement (which was partly successful because class differences "tended to play a less important function") have produced positive and negative consequences. Increased social mobility for some often translates into decreased social awareness and concern for the black community as a whole. As the sons and daughters of the black middle-class protagonists of the civil rights movement come of age, they are comprising a "Liberated Black Elite." This elite seems to have some initial guilt about denying their roots in a black subculture but are adjusting to the marginality that such denial and being black middle class in this society entails.[15] Consequently, they consciously (some black political and intellectual conservatives) and unconsciously (those in the black middle class who are struggling to maintain such status at whatever costs)[16] join the rest of society in writing off the black masses. Even black liberals who, in clinging to the moral vision of integration, regard present attempts to reclaim a functional separatism (e.g., establishment of separate public schools to educate black boys) as retrogressive are engaging in counter-liberative morality by ignoring that integration had and continues to have serious racist-classist consequences for some black people who were and are unable, by virtue of their lower-class position, to benefit from civil rights legislation. I raise this last point in order to suggest that the mediating process of the club women's ethic pushes us to recognize that:

> *The ideals of integration and nationalism are insufficient for the problems we now face and for the issues with which we will have to deal in the future. We need to do more than try to be assimilated into white American society or to separate ourselves from it. Neither alternative is possible or even desirable. We need a broader perspective, one that includes the creative values of both but also moves beyond them to an entirely new vision of the future.*[17]

This argument does not ignore those Blacks who are recent arrivals to the middle class and who continue to provide financial support for relatives who remain in poverty.[18] Rather, the contention is that all Blacks are enmeshed in a structure of social inequality such that the question of how to be a socially responsible community is equally important for all classes. There is a precarious quality to the social mobility which Blacks experience (e.g., the link between mobility and government policy).[19] All classes of Blacks, therefore, need to discern authentic responsibilities of interrelatedness and mutuality as members of an oppressed community within the context of racist and classist exploitation.

It is thus proposed here that a mediating ethic that has at least the elements of a vision of God's justice, a core value of intragroup social responsibility, and a logic of interstructured oppression offers a point of departure for ethical reflection on the dilemma deriving from stratification. From the vision, value, and logic of a mediating ethic, the socioreligious ethical imperative to overcome oppressive processes for the sake of reunion requires that black people begin ethical reflection upon the conditions creating the dilemma of social stratification within the black community as we struggle with the elements of intercommunal reconciliation. Blacks must acknowledge that we are estranged from one another by class divisions and interests derived not only from the macro oppressive situation but from its impact in the micro context. Class status rather than God has become the center of value for the community, thus creating the ethical dilemma of competitive individualism versus intragroup social responsibility. The black community is betraying the vision of God's justice and is thus responding out of distrust rather than trust or faith in God. With class status as the center of value, other values become disordered, and God's justice is subverted and undermined. At such a point, Blacks are unable to be responsible moral agents of liberative activity to which God's justice calls us.

The socioreligious mediating ethic pushes the black community to determine ethical principles for moral agency in light of our faith claims about God and liberation and our sociohistorical context. This means that when black persons consider present reality, an ethical principle such as the renunciation of privilege should become operative for morally responsible Blacks relative to the context(s) in which they find themselves. In the larger context of white racist, patriarchal, classist U.S. society, the principle of renunciation should have some *prima facie* status for how the upper- and middle-class Blacks render liberative ethical decisions and action in relation to lower classes of Blacks. The upper and middle classes must think about how to renounce privileges (to move from sympathy to empathy) that deny the interconnection with the lower classes. The aim is to reduce tensions and alienation, for reunion is essential for liberation. Upper- and middle-class Blacks must use the principle of renunciation of privilege as an ethical guide for a more directly participatory role in a black liberation movement to restructure radically the society in which we live. Simply put, we must ask ourselves what we are willing to return to the community or live without in order for all in the black community to live with dignity, have a place to live, secure life-sustaining employment, and genuinely love one another.[20]

In a context such as the black church, all classes of Blacks are required to renounce the worship of other gods (money, success, expensive cars, etc.). The black church itself as an institution must take seriously the challenge to be more a socioreligious movement along the lines of the paradigm of the black women's club movement. It must renounce its claims to be the institutional bulwark of black freedom struggles and engage more purposefully in coalitions with others within the community who do not share certain theological points of view.

The black church must become more the place where we gather as the people of God to undertake Bible study, prayer meeting, Sunday morning service, and evangelism in the community that derives from moral visions wherein the theological and the social analytical is mediated. In a mediating process, we should not fear loss of our theological center just because we take seriously different theological or nontheological strategies for black liberation. We should remember that we will be creating spaces for God's continuing revelation in the midst of our dialogue.

The principle of renunciation of privilege as it applies within the black church means that we as individuals within the church reaffirm the greater good of the community, striving to nurture character as well as to discern and fulfill obligations and duties to one another. The principle of renunciation of privilege in both the macro and micro contexts will aid us in making the hard ethical choices required by social stratification.

Finally, from their logic of interstructured oppression and sense of socioreligious ethical responsibility, the black club women found that they could never lose sight of the fact that they were bound to all classes of black women and black people, that alleviating gender oppression was a part of alleviating race and class oppression. Moreover, they understood the importance of both individual efforts and collective action. The paradigm for a mediating ethic embodied in the black women's club movement is the foundation for a socioreligious ethic for black liberation that affirms that black liberation will not occur apart from the eradication of race-gender-class oppression. Hard ethical choices will need to be made in light of sociohistorical, political, and economic realities that constitute the complexity of black oppression today. African Americans must choose to live into the tensions of the external and internal dimensions of black oppression and to seek to mediate between accommodative and aggressive political activism, between religious radicalism for and the socioeconomics of societal change, between progress for individual Blacks and progress for Blacks as a group. The vision of God's justice, intragroup social responsibility, and the logic of interstructured oppression deriving from the ethic of the black club women are the bases for a socioreligious mediating ethical process for black liberation that may truly be the way to overcome the depth of race-gender-class oppression. Thus it will provide the necessary content of an ethic for black liberation as well as a way to engage authentically in intercommunal reconciliation.

# 6

# Socioreligious Moral Vision for the Twenty-first Century

The black women's club movement of the late nineteenth and early twentieth centuries is a resource for confronting black oppression, particularly social stratification in the black community, and for intracommunal reunion. The club movement provides an ethical process, a process of mediating, and the paradigm of a thoroughly social *and* religious movement that brought thought and action, socioreligious praxis, to fruition. My contention in this final chapter is that the black club women's praxis is not only paradigmatic for black liberation ethical reflection, but can also move all of us in the church toward a liberative moral vision for the twenty-first century. This is a discussion of the meaning of the club women's perspective for intercommunal reconciliation.

Upon examination of the club movement as socioreligious praxis, I have found at the heart three key elements: *renunciation, inclusivity,* and *responsibility*. These elements, deriving from the club women's moral vision of God's justice and justice for the black community as a command of God, are critical for rethinking our ethical responses to interactive processes of oppression, best characterized as institutionalized moral evil, and for formulating a moral vision.

The first element, renunciation, recalls the ability of the black female elite to recognize their commonality, to create shared understanding, and to work with other classes of black women. We learn from the black women's club movement that our efforts to be in solidarity with persons or groups unlike ourselves does not derive from an ability to transcend the facts of difference (such as race, gender, class) but from our *willingness to renounce* (to give up, to refuse) the "privilege of difference." The "privilege of difference" denotes favor, advantage, or benefit resulting from and in socially constructed meanings of human worth that are exclusionary and divisive—and which are signs of institutionalized moral evil. In other words, we think ourselves better than others by social, political, and/or economic standards of valuation.

To renounce the "privilege of difference," to be and act as moral agents, is to discern that the morally relevant in our relationships does not derive from *some disembodied human essence* we share—that is, the assumption that we recognize one another's humanity when we ignore our embodied differences, such as female or male or white or black. The morally relevant derives instead from our *concrete embodiedness*—that is, the assumption that we must recognize and respect the particularities of one another.[1] A concrete embodiedness can engender inclusiveness and interrelationship whereas the assumption of disembodied human essence fosters exclusion and divisiveness, in that we have never learned to accept and respect our differences as good and as reflective of the likeness of God.

The virtue of the renunciation of privilege is, perhaps, akin to the Christian virtue of sacrifice in that both virtues require us to let go of something outside of or about ourselves that we value in order to attain a greater good ("Those who find their life will lose it, and those who lose their life for my sake will find it," Matt. 10:39). However, renunciation of privilege is distinguishable from sacrifice in that it qualifies some of our unhealthy understandings of that virtue. For example, one unhealthy understanding of sacrifice is that denial premised upon transcendence of embodiment (particularly those features of human existence that often are the source of tension and conflict) is the fullest expression of Christian morality, both individually and communally. Renunciation requires us to accept our embodiment and to acknowledge the way we humans confuse achieved worth or statuses with our created worthiness given by God the Creator and sustained through Jesus Christ the Redeemer. With such acceptance and acknowledgment, we can discern that achieved economic or educational status (difference of privilege) is sinful and a hindrance to Christian morality when it constitutes the whole of human worth. Renunciation may even help us to comprehend further what may seem paradoxical in the relationship between losing our lives for Christ's sake and finding them. That is, faithful followers of Christ (individually and communally) are those who use their achievements in answering a call to serve Christ and others, rather than as means for promoting themselves or structures that exclude those who do not have such achievements. Renunciation may require something as simple as listening rather than speaking when one has the most formal education in the setting; or, it may involve a more drastic choice such as leaving a lucrative job and its prestige for work more directly focused on transforming oppressive realities. Renunciation might also mean re-organizing the structure of an institution to include those who have not traditionally held positions of power.

The second element for a moral vision which we retrieve from the black club women is a sense of inclusivity. Inclusivity is a primary value and obligation of the black women's club movement. From the initial call to meet, which invited "all colored women of America, members of any society or not,"[2] to club work that addressed the diverse conditions and classes of black women, the NACW made inclusivity a moral good and duty. The black club women undertook their social reform efforts in terms of what they understood as the intrinsic connection between work on behalf of black women and all black people (the particular) and the greater good, reform of society aimed at justice for all (the universal).

From the club movement, we learn that inclusivity requires the removal of boundaries so as to realize interrelationship as a moral good. As obligation, it makes imperative not merely tolerating or seeking to overcome *but* respecting difference as the necessary point of departure for understanding and actualizing authentic unity. For example, intercommunal reconciliation between black people and white people necessitates that the boundaries of our different communities be malleable, allowing intercommunication and participation; but, unity between the groups will not occur by dissolving the boundaries. In other words, people of different racial-ethnic groups organizing themselves into separate movements and structures within and outside of the church are not in and of themselves signs of failure in the quest for unity in the body of Christ. Such separation is, however, a sign of moral failure when its sole purpose is exclusion, and differences are used to set us over and against one another.

Exclusionary separation is divisive; functional separatism recognizes differences as meaningful for interrelationships between groups; homogenization creates an artificial unity.

Functional separatism means that we accept the reality of our differences and may choose not to integrate. For example, we may cooperate in common endeavors toward racial justice, but without some ultimate reconciliation in view. We undertake these endeavors through a mediating ethical process. As mentioned earlier, mediating means *living in tension with* rather than aiming at an end result of integration, compromise, or reconciliation. A mediating ethical process is meant to suggest an alternative to making compromises. Unlike compromise, which can often be perceived either as an inability to take a definitive stand or a need to relinquish something in order to reach consensus, a mediating ethical process presents opportunities to create moral responses to moral dilemmas. The responses are open-ended and thus enable us to envision our moral life as a process, as the ability to live and act within the tensions of our moral dilemmas. Just as the club women were effective moral agents acting within the tensions of the moral dilemma of social stratification within the black community, we are called upon to mediate the tensions between integration and separatism if we desire to overcome the present impasse in race relations.

Equally important to the quest for inclusivity of groups is making our identity as social selves (individuals within groups) our normative, operative self-understanding. The women of the club movement revealed this self-understanding when they recognized that individual effort alone could not overcome the plight of black women and people as a group. A national movement thus became the vehicle for addressing their collective reality, "acting upon the principle of organization and union . . . to fulfill a mission to which they [felt] peculiarly adapted and especially called."[3]

The efforts of club women to fulfill a mission to which they felt peculiarly adapted and especially called signifies responsible moral agency on their part. Their efforts were "fitting" responses that mediated the fulfillment of their obligation and duty to racial uplift with their belief in God's justice. This meant that their mediating ethical process resulted in a moral vision of their religious responsibility. This same moral vision can move the church toward liberative moral agency and witness into the twenty-first century. Effective Christian moral vision and witness into the next century will depend on our ability to mediate the claims of particularity and the universal. In terms more specific to the church, it will depend on our ability to mediate denominationalism and ecumenism.

The club women's moral vision of social and religious responsibility sharpens for us what H. Richard Niebuhr meant when he wrote, "for the ethics of responsibility the *fitting* action . . . is alone conducive to the good and alone is right."[4] From the club women, we come to understand that fitting action grows out of mediating ethical processes in which neither our concern for the realities of our social context nor for our religious beliefs about who oversees that context subsumes the other. Rather, mediating our desire to correct injustices with our faith in a sovereign God is critical to moral vision and agency. The club women mediated the political and economic realities of their lives and their belief in a just God. There was an interacting dialogue between realities and their faith that enabled them to discern their fitting response to be the formation of a movement, the purpose of which was "by the help of God to secure harmony of action and cooperation among all women in raising to the highest plane, home, moral and civil life."[5] The club movement was, therefore, thoroughly social *and* religious.

Socioreligious praxis is the crux of a liberative moral vision for the church into the twenty-first century. The test of the vision will lie in its ability to sustain an alternative vision of reality from the normative vision premised upon ideologies of domination. In the case of the club women, their moral vision sustained a vision of reality that necessitated breaking with the normative vision of society (exclusionary separation) and even of the black community when that vision created complicity in, rather than accountability and responsibility for, overcoming oppressive realities. Their vision sustained a prophetic sensibility to moral evil, passion and compassion, historical consciousness, and communion with divine consciousness—in other words, it was grounded in their faith. From the club women we are admonished that moral vision that does not derive from experience and involve continuous intentional moral agency is deficient. From the club women we find direction toward a liberative moral vision for the next century in the cultivation of the virtue of renunciation of privilege, in striving for inclusivity as value and obligation, and in construing our ethical reflection as a mediating process. Moral agency defined as socioreligious praxis is critical. This is the understanding that we must grasp if our Christian ethics is to be more constructive than dogmatic—a mediating process of engaging and re-engaging, interpreting and reinterpreting, traditional and new sources for ethical reflection and moral agency. Using such a process I conclude this book with a sermonic fragment.

# 7

# A Sermonic Fragment

The concluding verse of 1 Corinthians 13 reads: "And now faith, hope, and love abide, these three; and the greatest of these is love."[1] Often this chapter and verse of Corinthians are used to assert that love is *the* final word on Christian morality. We can reconsider this assertion if we allow the traditional biblical source and the new source, the ethical insights of the black club women, to encounter each other through mediating process.

It is not that we should draw a direct analogy between renunciation, inclusivity, and responsibility, on one hand, and faith, hope, and love, on the other. Instead, what is important is the encounter between the sets of terms, compelling us to reinterpret and re-engage this familiar passage of scripture. Out of such reinterpretation and re-engagement, we may, perhaps, discern that the greatness of love is not that faith and hope are subsumed by it but that love is the center of a moral vision grasped only by those who are faithful and act out of hope. For, life is confusing and fragmentary ("now we see in a mirror dimly" and "know in part"), and the ability to mediate life's realities and the eschatological future when "we will see face to face" and "know fully" is critical. To mediate social realities, to be consistent and persistent (faithful), and to act in mercy, kindness, justice—for reasons that may or may not be articulated (to act out of hope)—is to live the Christian moral vision of love. Love does not, cannot, exist apart from being faithful and performing acts of hope; yet often we seem to suggest this when we make Christian love a virtue that denies the claims embodiment makes upon us—claims such as renunciation of privilege, inclusivity, and responsibility.

The Christian vision of love that takes seriously the claims of embodiment pushes us to live morally, to expect *kairos*-experiences wherein the Spirit breaks into our midst and reclaims us so that we can renounce the privilege of domination; so that we can commit ourselves to discovering untried (even unconventional) ways of gender, racial, economic, and theological inclusivity; and so that we can open ourselves to fitting responses to the realities of institutionalized moral evil. Living thus, we will begin a Christian ethical process of mediating intentional work to change oppressive realities with our faith in God in Jesus Christ who bestows grace as the assurance that we may attempt any such change at all.

# Notes

The title for this book is from an address given by Mrs. Carrie W. Clifford, president of the Ohio Federation of Colored Women's Clubs, reported in *Alexander's Magazine*, 15 August 1905. Mrs. Clifford said, "The spirit of club life shall be a clarion-call to Afro-American people to awake! arise! act!" It is hoped that this book captures the spirit of the club movement as it sounds anew that clarion call.

## Preface

1. Carol D. Stack, *All Our Kin: Strategies for Survival in a Black Community* (New York: Harper and Row, 1974), as cited in Patricia Hill Collins, *Black Feminist Thought* (New York: Routledge, 1990), 120.

2. I understand that the use of the terms "truths" and "facts" is problematic because it is critical to be aware of how they are interpreted and by whom and for what purposes. My understanding of these terms and social myths is derived from Elizabeth Janeway, *Man's World, Woman's Place: A Study in Social Mythology* (New York: Morrow, 1971).

3. See Walter G. Muelder, *Moral Law in Christian Social Ethics* (Richmond, Va.: John Knox Press, 1966), 20; Paul Deats, "The Quest for a Social Ethic," and James M. Gustafson, "The Relevance of Historical Understanding," *Toward a Discipline of Social Ethics,* ed. Paul Deats (Boston: Boston University Press, 1972), 21–48, 49–70; Glenn H. Stassen, "A Social Theory Model for Religious Social Ethics," *Journal of Religious Ethics* 5, no. 1 (1977): 9–37; Gibson Winter, *Elements for a Social Ethic* (New York: Macmillan, 1966) for examples of interdisciplinary approaches.

4. Beverly Harrison, "Theological Reflection in the Struggle for Liberation," *Making the Connections,* ed. Carol S. Robb (Boston: Beacon Press, 1985), 249.

5. Ibid., 249–59.

## Introduction

1. See Alice Walker, *In Search of Our Mothers' Gardens: Womanist Prose* (New York: Harcourt Brace Jovanovich, 1983), xi–xii, for a definition of "womanist" and "Roundtable Discussion: Christian Ethics and Theology in Womanist Perspective," *Journal of Feminist Studies in Religion* 5, no. 2 (fall 1989): 83–112, for a discussion of black female ethicists' and theologians' appropriation of Walker's term.

2. See Bruce C. Birch and Larry L. Rasmussen, *Bible and Ethics in the Christian Life* (Minneapolis: Augsburg, 1976), 82–83. Birch and Rasmussen identify the tasks of Christian ethics as descriptive (seeking to comprehend and describe the moral life as it is actually lived), critical (assessing the moral life), and normative (stating the content and procedures for living the moral life as it ought to be lived).

3. Manning Marable, *How Capitalism Underdeveloped Black America* (Boston: South End Press, 1983), 70.

4. Thomas C. Holt, "Introduction: Whither Now and Why?" *The State of Afro-American History: Past, Present, Future*, ed. Darlene Clark Hine (Baton Rouge: Louisiana State University Press, 1986), 2–3; and August Meier and Elliott Rudwick, eds., "On the Dilemmas of Scholarship in Afro-American History," *Black History and the Historical Profession, 1915–1980* (Urbana: University of Illinois Press, 1986), 299.

5. Meier and Rudwick, 236.

6. See Armstead L. Robinson, "The Difference Freedom Made: The Emancipation of Afro-Americans," and Kenneth L. Kusmer, "The Black Urban Experience in American History," *The State of Afro-American History*, 51–74, 91–122.

7. Sheila Ryan Johansson, "Herstory as History: A New Field or Another Fad," *Liberating Women's History*, ed. Bernice A. Carroll (Urbana: University of Illinois Press, 1976), 370–71. See also Gerda Lerner, *The Majority Finds Its Past: Placing Women in History* (New York: Oxford University Press, 1979), xiv.

8. Hilda Smith, "Feminism and the Methodology of Women's History," *Liberating Women's History*, 382–83. Smith notes that class is defined by an androcentric view of society and a woman's class (unless she is a single, self-supporting adult) is determined by the occupation of her husband. She suggests that we must pose questions and develop hypotheses that account for the restrictions upon women's lives (for example, the number of children is as determinative a factor in a woman's class as her husband's income).

9. Gerda Lerner, "Black Women in the United States: A Problem in Historiography and Interpretation," *The Majority Finds Its Past*, 73–74.

10. The term is borrowed from Bonnie Thornton Dill, "The Dialectics

of Black Womanhood," *Signs* 4, no. 3 (spring 1979): 543. See also Collins, *Black Feminist Thought*, 21–29. Collins offers a working definition of black feminist thought as "specialized knowledge created by African American women which clarifies a standpoint of and for Black women" and five key dimensions of a Black woman's standpoint: (1) a legacy of struggle; (2) web of experience shaping a diversity of responses; (3) interdependence of experience and consciousness; (4) struggle for a self-defined standpoint; and (5) interdependence of thought and action.

11. Albert R. Jonson, *Responsibility in Modern Religious Ethics* (Washington, D.C.: Corpus Books, 1968), 78, 176.

12. Katie G. Cannon, "Hitting a Straight Lick with a Crooked Stick: The Womanist Dilemma in the Development of a Black Liberation Ethic," *Annual of the Society of Christian Ethics* 1987: 168.

## I. A Sociology of Black Liberation

1. Gregory Baum, *The Social Imperative* (New York: Paulist Press, 1979), 148, 149, 151.

2. See Joyce A. Ladner, "Part III: Black Sociology: Toward a Definition of Theory," *The Death of White Sociology*, ed. Joyce A. Ladner (New York: Random House, 1973), 161–252; Robert Staples, "What Is Black Sociology? Toward a Sociology of Black Liberation," *The Death of White Sociology*, 162–63. See also Dennis Forsythe, "Radical Sociology and Blacks," *The Death of White Sociology*, 214, 216. Forsythe critiques mainstream American sociology as an "abstracted empiricism" based upon a commitment to "the ideal of neutrality, noncommitment, or objectivity."

3. Abd-l Hakimu Ibn Alkalimat (Gerald McWorter), "The Ideology of Black Social Science," *The Death of White Sociology*, 174.

4. Robert Staples, *Introduction to Black Sociology* (New York: McGraw-Hill, 1976), 3.

5. Staples, "What Is Black Sociology?" *The Death of White Sociology*, 168.

6. See studies such as Richard Sennett and Jonathan Cobb, *The Hidden Injuries of Class* (New York: Vintage Books, 1973), and Robert N. Bellah et al., *Habits of the Heart* (New York: Harper and Row, 1986), for studies on the impact of class in the larger society.

7. Beth Vanfossen, *The Structure of Social Inequality* (Boston: Little, Brown, 1979), 376, 9, 233. Cf. Oliver C. Cox, *Caste, Class, and Race* (Garden City, N.Y.: Doubleday, 1948), 148–51. Cox elaborates the notion of competitive class consciousness in a discussion of individualism as the ideology of the social class system.

8. Ibid., 52–54. Vanfossen adopts this model because she says that it

establishes a relationship between determinative institutions (economic and political systems) and supportive institutions (control and socialization systems) in the allocation of a society's resources.

9. The term "capitalist democracy" is borrowed from Joshua Cohen and Joel Rogers, *On Democracy: Toward a Transformation of American Society* (New York: Penguin Books, 1984), 49. Cohen and Rogers suggest that capitalism and democracy have so thoroughly merged that a completely new system exists.

10. Vanfossen, *The Structure of Social Inequality*, 202–203, 238–39, 201. The American ideology of egalitarianism "claims that there is great opportunity for social mobility, that anyone can succeed, that people get what they deserve, and that anyone can move from the bottom to the top if only he or she has the ambition and talent."

11. James E. Blackwell, *The Black Community: Diversity and Unity* (New York: Harper and Row, 1985), 119. See also Vanfossen, *The Structure of Social Inequality*, 202–3.

12. Blackwell, 119.

13. William Ryan, *Blaming the Victim* (New York: Vintage Books, 1976), 7–8. Ryan notes that the ideology of "blaming the victim" can emphasize the intrinsic defects of victims (a stigma of genetic origin marks the victims) and/or environmental causation (a stigma of social origin marks the victims). See also Reeve Vanneman and Lynn Weber Cannon, *The American Perception of Class* (Philadelphia: Temple University Press, 1987), 19–37. Vanneman and Cannon critique the psychological reductionism of class theory which ignores structural factors.

14. Joseph R. Gusfield, *Community: A Critical Response* (New York: Harper and Row, 1975), xv–xvi. The territorial or ecological usage takes account of factors such as location, physical territory, and geographical continuity or refers to "human aggregates distributed within certain ecological boundaries who share common experience, value systems, and social institutions." The relational or sociopsychological meaning "points to the quality or character of human relationships, without reference to location" and to "the role of shared values in creating a sense of identity with a particular group that may or may not live within the same geographic boundary."

15. Ibid., 29.

16. Ibid., 35, 36. Gusfield discusses a "consciousness of kind" and a sense of participating in the same history as well as the role of conflict and interaction with other groups as important in the emergence of a communal identity.

17. Daniel C. Thompson, *Sociology of the Black Experience* (Westport, Conn.: Greenwood Press, 1974), 39–43. Thompson discusses survival

(personally and as a socially conscious, viable group) as "the basic fact of black experience."

18. Blackwell, *The Black Community*, 5–10, 11–13, 13–14. Blackwell says that these constructs help provide better insights into the nature of collective responses that black Americans have made in the past and continue to make to the conditions of subjugation, discrimination, prejudice, and institutionalized racism. These collective responses are typified by individual reactions to external conditions imposed upon the community as a whole as well as to the internal affairs of the community itself. See also Staples, *Introduction to Black Sociology*, 14–16.

19. Blackwell, *The Black Community*, 119–26; also Staples, *Introduction to Black Sociology*, 76–78, 188–89.

20. Blackwell, *The Black Community*, 14. See Staples, *Introduction to Black Sociology*, 14.

21. Blackwell, *The Black Community*, 11–14, 119–20; Staples, *Introduction to Black Sociology*, 183.

22. Staples, *Introduction to Black Sociology*, 201. See also Richard T. Shaefer, *Racial and Ethnic Groups* (Boston: Little, Brown, 1979), 32–33, 57.

23. Blackwell, *The Black Community*, 14.

24. Richard Morris and Raymond Murphy, "A Paradigm for the Study of Class Consciousness," *Sociology and Social Research* 50 (April 1966): 310.

25. Ibid., 303, 310. Stratum consciousness is identification with, or commitment to, the interests and ideology of the stratum.

26. I am borrowing the term "contextual interactive" from Althea Smith and Abigail J. Stewart, "Approaches to Studying Racism and Sexism in Black Women's Lives," *Journal of Social Issues* 39 (1983): 1–2, 9–12. Smith and Stewart discuss the need for a contextual interactive research model for examining racism and sexism as dynamic processes that are independent as well as provide contexts for each other.

27. Marable, *How Capitalism Underdeveloped Black America*, 2.

28. James Turner, "The Sociology of Black Nationalism," *The Death of White Sociology*, 236.

## 2. The Race versus Class Debate

1. William J. Wilson, *The Declining Significance of Race: Blacks and Changing American Institutions*, 2d ed. (Chicago: University of Chicago Press, 1980), 150, 152.

2. Charles V. Willie, ed., "The Inclining Significance of Race," *Caste and Class Controversy* (Bayside, N.Y.: General Hall, 1979), 145–46.

3. Wilson, *The Declining Significance of Race*, 166.

4. Ibid. Wilson elaborates this discussion in his work, *The Truly Disadvantaged: The Inner City, the Underclass, and Public Policy* (Chicago: University of Chicago Press, 1987).

5. "Forum: Moving Up at Last?" *Harper's*, February 1987, 37.

6. Ibid.

7. Ibid., 44, 45.

8. Blackwell, *The Black Community*, 144–45.

9. Seymour Leventman, "Class and Ethnic Tensions: Minority group Leadership in Transition," *Sociology and Social Research* 50 (April 1966): 371–76.

10. Charles U. Smith, "The Black Middle Class and the Struggle for Civil Rights," *Black American* (New York: Basic Books, 1970), 230–40.

11. Sidney Kronus, *The Black Middle Class* (Columbus, Ohio: Charles E. Merrill, 1971), 132–33, 141.

12. Daniel C. Thompson, *A Black Elite* (New York: Greenwood Press, 1986), 3–4, 137, 138. Thompson says, "in this context the concept 'elite' refers specifically to individuals of talents and achievements who may have come from all of the socioeconomic levels and social classes in the black community from which United Negro College Fund–related colleges recruit their students." See also Kenneth B. Clark, *Dark Ghetto: Dilemmas of Social Power* (New York: Harper and Row, 1965), 55–58. Clark describes this attitude among upwardly mobile Blacks as "presenting an apology for oppression."

13. Reynolds Farley, *Blacks and Whites: Narrowing the Gap?* (Cambridge, Mass.: Harvard University Press, 1984), 172–88.

14. Ibid., 188–202; Vanneman and Cannon, *The American Perception of Class*, 225–51. See also William A. Sampson, "New Insights on Middle Class Mobility," *Urban League Review* 5 (summer 1980): 21–41; Bart Landry, *The New Black Middle Class* (Berkeley: University of California Press, 1987).

15. Douglas G. Glasgow, *The Black Underclass* (New York: Vintage Books, 1981).

16. See Cornel West, *Race Matters* (Boston: Beacon Press, 1993), chapters 2–4, and "Unmasking the Black Conservatives," *Christian Century*, 16–23 July 1986, 644–48; Joseph G. Conti and Brad Stetson, *Challenging the Civil Rights Establishment: Profiles of a New Black Vanguard* (Westport, Conn.: Praeger, 1993); Manning Marable, *How Capitalism Underdeveloped Black America* (Boston: South End Press, 1983), chapter 6; Bernard Boxill, *Blacks and Social Justice* (Totowa, N.J.: Rowman and Allanheld, 1984), chapters 2 and 8, for discussions that elaborate my generalized remarks.

17. This dilemma should not be understood as unrelated to three enduring ethical dilemmas in the external dimension of black oppression: (1) economic expediency versus socioeconomic and moral justice; (2)

white supremacy versus racial inclusiveness; and (3) complicity versus responsibility for overcoming oppression. See my essay, "Ethics for Living a Dream Deferred," *Drew Gateway* (fall 1989): 3–21, for a fuller discussion.

18. See Gayraud S. Wilmore, *Black Religion and Black Radicalism* (Maryknoll, N.Y.: Orbis Books, 1983), 168. "Basically [black radicalism] has been a homegrown, race-conscious, unsystematic attack on the roots of black misery in American life—racism." I am using the term "religious radicalism" to imply a form of radicalism such as is expressed in black theology.

19. See Oliver C. Cox, *Caste, Class, and Race* (Garden City, N.Y.: Doubleday, 1948), 571. Cox says, "Two principle ideas of racial policy seem to divide the allegiance of Negroes, the one, that 'Negroes should stick together' and the other, that 'Negroes should shift for themselves individually since the individual can advance more easily than the group as a whole.' In reality, however, these two plans of action are correlated. The first is a necessity, the second an aspiration."

## 3. Roots of the Dilemma (1800–1920)

1. Bureau of the Census, *The Social and Economic Status of the Black Population in the United States: An Historical View, 1790–1978*, Special Studies, series P-23, no. 8 (Washington, D.C.: U.S. Department of Commerce, 1979), ix. See also John Hope Franklin and Alfred A. Moss, Jr., *From Slavery to Freedom: A History of Negro Americans* (6th ed.; New York: Knopf, 1988), 112–13; Reynolds Farley and Walter Allen, *The Color Line and the Quality of Life in America* (New York: Russell Sage, 1987), 11–12.

2. Benjamin Quarles, *The Negro in the Making of America* (2d rev. ed.; New York: Collier Books, 1987), 70. See also Franklin and Moss, *From Slavery to Freedom*, 117; E. Franklin Frazier, *The Negro in the United States* (New York: Macmillan, 1949), 275. Frazier suggests that there were even distinctions in rank among the house servants with reference to the level of responsibility associated with a position or whether the position brought one into a relationship of confidence with the master.

3. Franklin and Moss, *From Slavery to Freedom*, 122, 137; Quarles, 69. See also W. E. B. DuBois, "The Ante-Bellum Negro Artisan," *The Other Slaves: Mechanics, Artisans and Craftsmen*, ed. James E. Newton and Ronald L. Lewis (Boston: G. K. Hall, 1978), 175–82.

4. See John W. Blassingame, *The Slave Community: Plantation Life in the Antebellum South* (2d ed.; New York: Oxford University Press, 1979), and Eugene D. Genovese, *Roll, Jordan, Roll: The World the Slaves Made* (New York: Vintage Books, 1976), for accounts that support the notion of the slave population as a parallel community.

5. Mary Frances Berry and John W. Blassingame, *Long Memory: The Black Experience in America* (New York: Oxford University Press, 1982), 30.

6. John W. Blassingame, "Status and Social Structure in the Slave Community," *The Afro-American Slaves: Community or Chaos*, ed. Randall M. Miller (Malabar, Fla.: Robert E. Krieger Publishing Co., 1981), 112.

7. Ibid., 120–21. Compare Kenneth M. Stampp, *The Peculiar Institution* (New York: Knopf, 1978), 333–36.

8. August Meier and Elliott Rudwick, *From Plantation to Ghetto* (rev. ed.; New York: Hill and Wang, 1970), 101.

9. There were approximately a half million free Blacks by 1860, and, as a group, they tended to reside in urban areas. Ibid., Meier and Rudwick, 73; Frazier, *The Negro in the United States*, 66.

10. Frazier, *The Negro in the United States*, 59; Franklin and Moss, *From Slavery to Freedom*, 136–37; Quarles, *The Negro in the Making of America*, 83–85. See also Ira Berlin, *Slaves Without Masters: The Free Negro in the Antebellum South* (New York: Pantheon Books, 1974), 15–132.

11. Frazier, *The Negro in the United States*, 70.

12. Franklin and Moss, *From Slavery to Freedom*, 144. See also Rayford W. Logan, *The Negro in American Life and Thought: The Nadir, 1877–1901* (New York: Dial, 1954), 118–19.

13. Quarles, *The Negro in the Making of America*, 89, 93–94. See also Logan, *The Nego in American Life and Thought*, 118. "[Free Negroes] worked in fifty different occupations in Charleston and in more than seventy in North Carolina. In the slave state of Maryland, some 2,000 free Negroes of Baltimore engaged in nearly one hundred occupations, including paperhanging, engraving, quarrying, photography and tailoring. New Orleans had colored jewelers, architects and lithographers."

14. Quarles, *The Negro in the Making of America*; Logan, *The Negro in American Life and Thought*, 119.

15. Quarles, *The Negro in the Making of America*, 91–92; John W. Blassingame, *Black New Orleans: 1860–1880* (Chicago: University of Chicago Press, 1973), 21–22; Frazier, *The Negro in the United States*, 77–78.

16. Frazier, *The Negro in the United States*, 275.

17. Berry and Blassingame, *Long Memory*, 37.

18. Meier and Rudwick, *From Plantation to Ghetto*, 101; Logan, *The Negro in American Life and Thought*, 118.

19. Ronald T. Takaki, *Iron Cages: Race and Culture in Nineteenth Century America* (New York: Knopf, 1979), 110.

20. Quarles, *The Negro in the Making of America*, 86–88, 92–93; Berlin, *Slaves Without Masters*, 182–216, 316–40. See also Leonard P. Curry, *The Free Black in Urban America, 1800–1850: The Shadow of the Dream* (Chicago: University of Chicago Press, 1981), 15–36, 81–95.

21. Takaki, *Iron Cages*, 122–23. See also W. E. B. DuBois, *Black Reconstruction* (New York: Harcourt, Brace, 1935), chapters 2–3.

22. See Franklin and Moss, *From Slavery to Freedom*, 113: "In 1860, there were approximately 8 million whites, but there were only 384,884 owners of slaves. Thus, fully three-fourths of the white people of the South had neither slaves nor an immediate economic interest in the maintenance of slavery or the plantation system. And yet, the institution came to dominate the political and economic thinking of the entire South and to shape its social pattern for two principal reasons. The great majority of the staple crops were produced on plantations employing slave labor, thus giving the owners an influence out of proportion to their numbers. Then there was the hope on the part of most of the nonslaveholders that they would some day become owners of slaves. Consequently, they took on the habits and patterns of thought of the slaveholders before they actually joined that select class."

23. Takaki, *Iron Cages*, 116.

24. Ibid., 111.

25. See Genovese, *Roll, Jordan, Roll*, 327–98, and Stampp, *The Peculiar Institution*, 331–40, for discussions that point out the ambiguities and tensions within the slave community because of stratification.

26. See Berlin, *Slaves Without Masters*, 217–83, and Curry, *The Free Black in Urban America*, 15–36, 81–95, for discussions and data to support this characterization of the economic status of and class relationships within the free black community.

27. See Curry, *The Free Black in Urban America*, chapter 12; Howard Holman Bell, *A Survey of the Negro Convention Movement (1830–1861)* (New York: Arno Press, New York Times, 1969).

28. See Meier and Rudwick, *From Plantation to Ghetto*, 102–12; Berry and Blassingame, *Long Memory*, 52–69.

29. Wilson Jeremiah Moses, *The Golden Age of Black Nationalism, 1850–1925* (New York: Oxford University Press, 1978), 10–11, 32–50. See also Sterling Stuckey, *The Ideological Origins of Black Nationalism* (Boston: Beacon Press, 1972), 1–29, for an alternative interpretation.

30. Sterling Stuckey, *Slave Culture: Nationalist Theory and the Foundations of Black America* (New York: Oxford University Press, 1987), 198–231. Compare Berry and Blassingame, *Long Memory*, 389–91.

31. See, for example, Thomas Holt, *Black Over White: Negro Political Leadership in South Carolina During Reconstruction* (Urbana: University of Illinois Press, 1977), 42–71, for a discussion of the antebellum origins of black leadership in South Carolina that supports this assertion. See also Berry and Blassingame, 154, who note that urban slaves, blacksmiths, carpenters, clerks, or waiters in hotels and boardinghouses, some favored body servants of influential whites, preachers, lawyers, or teach-

ers in free states, and self-educated free men comprised the black leadership during Reconstruction.

32. Berlin, *Slaves Without Masters*, 388–89; also Blassingame, *Black New Orleans*, 155.

33. Berlin, *Slaves Without Masters*, 390.

34. See DuBois, *Black Reconstruction*, 123.

35. Berlin, *Slaves Without Masters*, 391–92.

36. Logan, *The Negro in American Life and Thought*, 327. See also George Washington Williams, *History of the Negro Race in America, 1619–1880* (New York: Arno Press, New York Times, 1968), 385–96.

37. Peter Camejo, *Racism, Revolution, Reaction, 1861–1877: The Rise and Fall of Radical Reconstruction* (New York: Monad, 1976), 91. See also Franklin and Moss, *From Slavery to Freedom*, 214. Compare Manning Marable, "The Land Question in Historical Perspective," *Blackwater: Historical Studies in Race, Class Consciousness, and Revolution* (Dayton, Ohio: Black Praxis Press, 1981), 54: "Through skill and determination . . . hundreds of thousands of black men did purchase what land was available to them. According to statistics of the Georgia comptroller general, the 83,318 black men who were registered to vote in 1874 owned 338,769 acres of land valued at $1.2 million. Their taxable property was worth $6.2 million, and virtually all had been slaves only a single decade before."

38. The following discussion relies heavily upon the class analysis of this period as presented in Camejo, *Racism, Revolution, Reaction;* Jack M. Bloom, *Class, Race, and the Civil Rights Movement* (Bloomington: Indiana University Press, 1987), chapter 1; and DuBois, *Black Reconstruction*.

39. Camejo, *Racism, Revolution, and Reaction*, 87–90; Bloom, *Class, Race, and the Civil Rights Movement*, 28–30.

40. Bloom, *Class, Race, and the Civil Rights Movement*, 19–20.

41. See Bloom, *Class, Race, and the Civil Rights Movement*, 31–36; Camejo, *Racism, Revolution, and Reaction*, 139–46, 158–68, 188–204; DuBois, *Black Reconstruction*, chapter 16; Franklin and Moss, *From Slavery to Freedom*, 227–31; Quarles, *The Negro in the Making of America*, 138–42; Meier and Rudwick, *From Plantation to Ghetto*, 176. See also Williams, *History of the Negro Race in America*, chapters 21 and 27.

42. Bloom, *Class, Race, and the Civil Rights Movement*, 20, 32. Compare Nell Irwin Painter, *Exodusters: Black Migration to Kansas After Reconstruction* (New York: Knopf, 1977), 66–67: "In the view of most articulate Southern whites, . . . the agricultural economy of the region formed an integrated whole, a scheme in which well-to-do whites, 'the wealth and intelligenista of the South,' were to oversee the development of the entire region. Poorer whites were to act as their helpmates, not decision makers, filling the roles of employee and policeman. Nor were Blacks to

function as political or economic autonomies but rather as faceless, docile laborers. According to this arrangement, elaborated from the top, each group worked in a smoothly running agricultural machine. This vision of Southern life nourished the endlessly repeated New South concept of the 'identity of interests' of all the units of the Southern economy. It was the keynote of the planter-dominated Vicksburg Labor Convention of 1879."

43. Stephen Steinberg, *The Ethnic Myth: Race, Ethnicity, and Class in America* (Boston: Beacon Press, 1981), 176–81.

44. Ibid. See also Meier and Rudwick, *From Plantation to Ghetto*, 154–55; Camejo, *Racism, Revolution, and Reaction*, 95–96.

45. Steinberg, *The Ethnic Myth*, 173.

46. Painter, *Exodusters*, 6–7; Camejo, *Racism, Revolution, and Reaction*, 91, 188–206; DuBois, *Black Reconstruction*, chapter 8; Williams, *History of the Negro Race in America*, 529–43.

47. Berlin, *Slaves Without Muscles*, 395.

48. See Holt, *Black Over White*, chapter 3.

49. Ibid., chapter 6; Berry and Blassingame, *Long Memory*, 156–57. Compare Leon F. Litwack, *Been in the Storm So Long: The Aftermath of Slavery* (New York: Knopf, 1979), 502–24.

50. August Meier, *Negro Thought in America: 1880–1915* (Ann Arbor, Mich.: Ann Arbor Paperbacks, 1966), 15. Compare Litwack, 531.

51. Painter, *Exodusters*, 14.

52. See Joe M. Richardson, *Christian Reconstruction: The American Missionary Association and Southern Blacks: 1861–1890* (Athens: University of Georgia Press, 1986), 37–53, for support of this assertion.

53. Stuckey, *Slave Culture*, 231–37; see also Litwack, *Been in the Storm So Long*, 540–42.

54. Howard N. Rabinowitz, *Race Relations in the Urban South, 1865–1890* (New York: Oxford University Press, 1978), 22–23.

55. Litwack, *Been in the Storm So Long*, 310–13.

56. Rabinowitz, *Race Relations in the Urban South*, 63, 78–96; Litwack, *Been in the Storm So Long*, 320, 367.

57. Rabinowitz, *Race Relations*, 240–44. See also Blassingame, *Black New Orleans*, 139–71. In addition to the differences noted by Rabinowitz, Blassingame contrasts the content and form of the religious services of the churches of the lower class with those of the upper class as indicative of social stratification. See especially 151–52.

58. Rabinowitz, *Race Relations in the Urban South*, 243–44, 97–123. See also Litwack, *Been in the Storm So Long*, 310–11; Meier and Rudwick, *From Plantation to Ghetto*, 215; Berlin, *Slaves Without Masters*, 253–55.

59. Rabinowitz, *Race Relations in the Urban South*, 95–96.

60. See Painter, *Exodusters*, 108–17. See also Franklin and Moss, *From*

*Slavery to Freedom,* 253; Bennett, *Before the Mayflower,* 271–72; Quarles, *The Negro in the Making of America,* 158; Williams, *History of the Negro Race in America,* 529–43. Some of the other states to which Blacks migrated were Missouri, Nebraska, Iowa, and Oklahoma.

61. Florette Henri, *Black Migration: Movement North, 1900–1920* (New York: Anchor Press, 1975), 1.

62. Ibid., 51. Bennett, *Before the Mayflower,* 344, cites these statistics on the migration of Blacks from plantations to cities in the South and North: first wave (between 1910 and 1920), 300,000; second wave (between 1920 and 1930), 1,300,00; third wave (1930), 1,500,00; fourth wave (1940), 2,500,00. Farley and Allen, *The Color Line and the Quality of Life in America* 112–13, note that during World War II and the two following decades there was a net movement of almost 1.5 million Blacks to the North and West.

63. Henri, *Black Migration,* 52–58.

64. Ibid., 92. See also W. E. B. DuBois, *The Philadelphia Negro* (Philadelphia: University of Pennsylvania, 1899), and *The Black North in 1901: A Social Study* (New York: Arno Press, New York Times, 1969), in which he discusses the impact of southern migrants upon the lives of Blacks in New York, Philadelphia, and Boston.

65. David M. Katzman, *Before the Ghetto: Black Detroit in the Nineteenth Century* (Urbana: University of Illinois Press, 1973), 135–46. Henri, *Black Migration,* 188–189, describes "elite Negro enclaves" (such as the Negro Society of the Sons of New York), which southern migrants found in Philadelphia, Chicago, and other northern cities. "These people did not agitate for political or legal relief from discrimination; they counted on building their own exclusive social, civic, and economic institutions. Like any white immigrant group that has established itself in American society, the entrenched black elite on the whole furiously resented the intrusion of uncouth new arrivals from the South who crowed into their cities and raised ghetto barriers where none had been before."

66. Landry, *The New Black Middle Class,* 29–36. See also E. Franklin Frazier, *The Negro Family in the United States* (New York: Dryden Press, 1948), 295–313.

67. Henri, *Black Migration,* 190–91.

68. Ibid., 62, 70. The deep south was especially effected by black migration. For example, "between 1910 and 1920 Mississippi suffered a loss of 129,600 blacks, Louisiana a loss of 180,800."

69. George M. Frederickson, *The Black Image in the White Mind* (Middletown, Conn.: Wesleyan University Press, 1987), 198–255.

70. Ibid., 258–62.

71. Ibid., 262–82; Bloom, *Class, Race, and the Civil Rights Movement,* 39–44; C. Vann Woodward, *The Strange Career of Jim Crow* (3d rev. ed.;

New York: Oxford University Press, 1974), 67–109. See Ray Stannard Baker, *Following the Color Line: American Negro Citizenship in the Progressive Era* (New York: Harper and Row, 1964), 3–25, for a discussion of the 1906 race riot in Atlanta.

72. Frederickson, *The Black Image in the White Mind*, 283–96: "[The Southern Progressive alternative] constituted no real break with the fundamentals of racist ideology but attempted rather to bring that ideology into harmony with such conservative goals as law and order, social harmony, and rule by a benevolent elite."

73. Ibid., 298–304, 311–12.

74. See Baker, *Following the Color Line*, 109–34; Steinberg, *The Ethnic Myth*, 201–7; Henri, *Black Migration*, 146–55, 85–87.

75. See Meier, *Negro Thought*, 42, 149.

76. This discussion of Booker T. Washington is based upon William Toll, *The Resurgence of Race: Black Social Theory from Reconstruction to the Pan-African Conferences* (Philadelphia: Temple University Press, 1979), chapter 2 and p. 48. See also Moses, *The Golden Age of Black Nationalism*, 91–98; August Meier, "Negro Class Structure and Ideology in the Age of Booker T. Washington," *Phylon* 23, no. 3: 258–66.

77. See the discussion of W. E. B. DuBois in Toll, *The Resurgence of Race*, chapters 3 and 4. See also Moses, *The Golden Age of Black Nationalism*, chapter 6; Stuckey, *Slave Culture*, chapter 5.

78. Stuckey, *Slave Culture*, 239.

## 4. Black Women's Perspective on the Dilemma

1. Hazel V. Carby, *Reconstructing Womanhood* (New York: Oxford University Press, 1987), 25. See also Paula Giddings, *When and Where I Enter: The Impact of Black Women on Race and Sex in America* (New York: William Morrow, 1984), 47, 49. Compare Catherine Clinton, *The Other Civil War: American Women in the Nineteenth Century* (New York: Hill and Wang, 1984), 34, who notes that even most upper-class and middle-class white women were not completely exempt from domestic labor and that if it was not required of them, they substituted other women's labor for their own.

2. Clinton, *The Other Civil War*, 18, 19.

3. Jacqueline Jones, *Labor of Love, Labor of Sorrow* (New York: Vintage Books, 1986), 12. Compare Clinton, *The Other Civil War*, 35.

4. See Angela Davis, *Women, Race, and Class* (New York: Random House, 1981), 5–10, 24. See also Bell Hooks, *Ain't I a Woman: Black Women and Feminism* (Boston: South End Press, 1981), chapter 1; Deborah Gray White, *Arn't I a Woman? Female Slaves in the Plantation South* (New York: W. W. Norton, 1985), chapter 2; Katie G. Cannon, *Black Womanist Ethics*

(Atlanta: Scholars Press, 1988), 31–41; Clinton, *The Other Civil War,* 34–35.

5. White, *Arn't I a Woman?* 29, 49, 61.

6. Sharon Harley, "Northern Black Female Workers: Jacksonian Era," *The Afro-American Woman: Struggles and Images,* ed. Sharon Harley and Rosalyn Terborg-Penn (Port Washington, N.Y.: Kennikat Press, 1978), 10; see also Clinton, *The Other Civil War,* 32–33.

7. Clinton, *The Other Civil War,* 33. Compare Eleanor Flexner, *Century of Struggle* (Cambridge, Mass.: Harvard University Press, 1975), 95.

8. Darlene Hine and Kate Wittenstein, "Female Slave Resistance: The Economics of Sex," *The Black Woman Cross-Culturally,* ed. Filomina Chioma Steady (Cambridge, Mass.: Schenkman, 1981), 289–99. See also Giddings, *When and Where I Enter,* 39–40; Lerone Bennett, Jr., "No Crystal Stair: The Black Woman in History," *Ebony* 32 (August 1977): 164–70.

9. See Bettina Aptheker, "Abolitionism, Woman's Rights, and the Battle Over the Fifteenth Amendment," *Woman's Legacy* (Amherst: University of Massachusetts Press, 1982), 19; Giddings, *When and Where I Enter,* 49–50; Flexner, *Century of Struggle,* 42. Curry, *The Free Black in Urban America,* chapter 12, distinguishes between these types of societies as follows: benevolent societies secured donations from the more affluent Negroes and dispensed the funds to assist some specific less-favored group in the black community (e.g., widows and orphans); beneficial societies organized the limited resources of the poor and provided for mutual support (e.g., payments in the event of unemployment, illness, or death of their members); literary societies worked for moral, cultural, and intellectual enhancement through library associations, debating societies, lyceums, and organizations devoted to public speaking, writing, and the study of literature. Curry also notes that each of these societies frequently served dual purposes (for example, literary societies often engaged in benevolent work).

10. Jones, *Labor of Love,* 59.

11. Holt, *Black Over White,* 35.

12. Giddings, *When and Where I Enter,* 63; Jones, *Labor of Love,* 70–72.

13. Hooks, *Ain't I a Woman,* 56–60; Davis, *Women, Race, and Class,* chapter 11.

14. Davis, *Woman, Race, and Class,* 87–88.

15. As in chapter 3, this discussion focuses upon migration to southern and northern cities rather than westward migration because of the greater numbers. See Lawrence B. de Graaf, "Race, Sex, and Region: Black Women in the American West, 1850–1920," *Pacific Historical Review* 49, no. 2 (May 1980): 285–313, for an account of the black woman's experience in the West, particularly the Rocky Mountain and Pacific Coast states.

16. Kelly Miller, "Surplus Negro Women," *Radicals and Conservatives* (New York: Schocken, 1968), 183.

17. Jones, *Labor of Love*, 73, 113, 74; Dolores Janiweski, "Sisters Under Their Skins: Southern Working Women, 1880–1950," *Sex, Race, and the Role of Women in the South*, ed. Joan V. Hawks and Sheila L. Skemp (Jackson: University of Mississippi Press, 1983), 20. See also Sharon Harley, "Black Women in a Southern City: Washington, D.C., 1890–1920," *Sex, Race, and the Role of Women*, 62. Harley also thinks that race is the overriding determinative factor in clerical employment because that there was only about a 7 percent difference in the literacy rate of black and native-born white women but a more than 90 percent difference between the number of black and white women occupying clerical positions in 1920.

18. Henri, *Black Migration*, 54, 61–62.

19. Marilyn Richardson, *Black Women and Religion: A Bibliography* (Boston: G. K. Hall, 1980), xv. Also Jualyane E. Dodson and Cheryl Townsend Gilkes, "Something Within: Social Change and Collective Endurance in the Sacred World of Black Christian Women," in *The Nineteenth Century*, vol. 1, *Women and Religion in America*, ed. Rosemary Ruether and Rosemary Keller (San Francisco: Harper and Row, 1979), 81, assert, "If anything characterizes the role of black women in religion in America, it is the successful extension of their individual sense of regeneration, release, redemption, and spiritual liberation to a collective ethos of struggle for and with the entire black community."

20. Dorothy Sterling, ed., *We Are Your Sisters: Black Women in the Nineteenth Century* (New York: W. W. Norton, 1984), 151.

21. Maria W. Stewart, *Productions of Mrs. Maria W. Stewart Presented to the First African Baptist Church and Society of the City of Boston* (Boston: Friends of Freedom and Virtue, 1835). Also Maria W. Stewart, "Religion and the Pure Principles of Morality, The Sure Foundation on Which We Must Build (1831)," reprinted in *Maria W. Stewart, America's First Black Woman Political Writer*, ed. Marilyn Richardson (Bloomington: Indiana University Press, 1987), 39.

22. Anna J. Cooper, "The Ethics of the Negro Question," address delivered at the biennial session of Friends' General Conference, Asbury Park, N.J., 5 September 1902, Anna J. Cooper Papers, Manuscript Division, Moorland-Spingarn Research Center, Howard University, Washington, D.C., 5–6.

23. As cited in Milton Meltzer, ed., *The Black Americans: A History in Their Own Words* (New York: Harper and Row, 1984), 145–48.

24. From *Religious Experience and Journal of Mrs. Jarena Lee, Giving an Account of Her Call to Preach the Gospel (1849)* as cited in Bert James Loewenberg and Ruth Bogin, eds., *Black Women in Nineteenth-Century American Life: Their Words, Their Thoughts, Their Feelings* (University Park:

Pennsylvania State University Press, 1976), 139.

25. Julia A. J. Foote, "A Brand Plucked from the Fire," *Sisters of the Spirit: Three Black Women's Autobiographies of the Nineteenth Century,* ed. William L. Andrews (Bloomington: Indiana University Press, 1986), 207.

26. William L. Andrews, ed., *Sisters of the Spirit* (Bloomington: Indiana University Press, 1986), 20.

27. Stewart, "Religion and the Pure Principles of Morality," *Maria W. Stewart,* 38.

28. Stewart, "An Address Delivered Before the Afric/American Female Intelligence Society," *Maria W. Stewart,* 53.

29. As cited in Meltzer, *The Black Americans,* 67–68.

30. Nannie H. Burroughs, "Not Color but Character," *Voice of the Negro* 1, no. 7 (July 1904): 277–79.

31. Judith Papachristou, "Associationism and Reform: 1890–1920," *Women Together* (New York: Knopf, 1976), 113.

32. Ibid.; Flexner, *Century of Struggle,* 182–83.

33. See Giddings, *When and Where I Enter,* chapter 6; Cynthia Neverdon-Morton, *Afro-American Women of the South and the Advancement of the Race, 1895–1925* (Knoxville: University of Tennessee Press, 1989), chapter 10; Floris Loretta Barnett Cash, "Womanhood and Protest: The Club Movement Among Black Women, 1892–1922" (Ph.D. diss., State University of New York at Stony Brook, 1986), 1–20.

34. This understanding of social movement is adapted from Naomi Rosenthal et al., "Social Movements and Network Analysis: A Case Study of Nineteenth-Century Women's Reform in New York State," *American Journal of Sociology* 90, no. 5 (1985): 1022–23.

35. Neverdon-Morton, *Afro-American Women of the South,* 193.

36. Ibid., 193, 198, 202, 206.

37. Fannie Barrier Williams, "The Club Movement Among Colored Women of America," *A New Negro for a New Century* (New York: Arno Press, 1969), 383. Emily H. Williams, "The National Association of Colored Women," *Southern Workman* 43 (September 1914): 481; compare Cheryl Townsend Gilkes, "The Role of Women in the Sanctified Church," *Journal of Religious Thought* 43 (spring-summer 1986): 35.

38. See Jane Cunningham Croly, *The History of the Woman's Club Movement in America* (New York: Henry G. Allen, 1898), and Karen J. Blair, *The Clubwoman as Feminist: True Womanhood Redefined, 1868–1914* (New York: Holmes and Meier, 1980).

39. See Sheila Rothman, *Woman's Proper Place: A History of Changing Ideals and Practices, 1870 to the Present* (New York: Basic Books, 1978), p. 5, chapters 2 and 3.

40. *A History of the Club Movement Among the Colored Women of the United States of America* (Washington, D.C.: National Association of Col-

ored Women's Clubs, Inc., 1902; reprinted, 1978), 3–5 (emphasis added); Charles Harris Wesley, *The History of the National Association of Colored Women's Clubs: A Legacy of Service* (Washington, D.C.: Mercury Press, 1984), 29–30.

41. Giddings, *When and Where I Enter*, 95; Davis, *Women, Race, and Class*, 134. Gerda Lerner, "Women's Rights and American Feminism," *The Majority Finds Its Past: Placing Women in History* (New York: Oxford University Press, 1979), 52, suggests that all such women's movements are dependent on a class of educated women with leisure.

42. Davis, *Women, Race, and Class*, 129–30.

43. Gerda Lerner, "Early Community Work of Black Club Women," *Journal of Negro History* 59 (1974): 167. Also see Ruth Hill, "Lifting As We Climb: Black Women's Organizations, 1890 to 1935," *Radcliffe Quarterly* 70 (March 1984): 25.

44. My interpretation differs from those that tend to stress the problems of elitism among the club leaders. See, for example, Evelyn Brooks Higginbotham, *Righteous Discontent: The Women's Movement in the Black Baptist Church, 1880–1920* (Cambridge, Mass.: Harvard University Press, 1993), 206–7, for a discussion that challenges my interpretation.

45. Giddings, *When and Where I Enter*, 98. Also see Tullia K. Brown Hamilton, "The National Association of Colored Women, 1896–1920" (Ph.D. diss., Emory University, 1978), chapter 2. Hamilton gives a composite biographical profile of black club women that provides supportive insights for Giddings's assertion.

46. Hine, "Lifting the Veil, Shattering the Silence: Black Women's History in Slavery and Freedom," *The State of Afro-American History*, 238.

47. Williams, "The Club Movement Among Colored Women of America," *A New Negro for a New Century*, 382–83.

48. *History of the Club Movement*, 44–45.

49. See Mary Church Terrell, *A Colored Woman in a White World* (Washington, D.C.: Randell, 1940).

50. Elizabeth Davis, *Lifting As They Climb: The National Association of Colored Women* (Washington, D.C.: National Association of Colored Women, 1933), 17–19.

51. Subject Files, National Association of Colored Women, 1897–1962, Mary Church Terrell Papers, Manuscript Division, Library of Congress, Washington, D.C.; *Minutes of the National Association of Colored Women, Held in Howard Chapel Congregational Church, at Nashville, Tenn., September 15th, 16th, 17th, and 18th, 1897* (Washington, D.C.: Smith Brothers Printers, 1901), 6, 12; Wesley, *The History of the National Association*, 42.

52. Mary Church Terrell Papers, Manuscript Department, Moorland-Spingarn Research Center, Howard University, Washington, D.C.

53. Hamilton, "The National Association," 55.

54. Subject Files, National Association of Colored Women, 1897–1962, Mary Church Terrell Papers, Manuscript Division, Library of Congress, Washington, D.C.

55. Nannie H. Burroughs, "The Colored Woman and Her Relation to the Domestic Problem," *The United Negro: His Problems and His Progress*, ed. I. Garland Penn and J. W. E. Bowen (Atlanta: D. E. Luther Publishing, 1902; reprinted, New York: Negro Universities Press, 1969), 324–29.

56. Fannie Barrier Williams, "An Extension of the Conference Spirit," *Voice of the Negro* 1 (July 1904): 300–303.

57. Williams, "The National Association," 482.

58. "Some Efforts of Negroes for Their Own Betterment," *The Atlanta University Publications*, ed. W. E. B. DuBois (Atlanta: Atlanta University Press, 1898), 59–60.

59. Wesley, *The History of the National Association*, 43; *Minutes of the National Association of Colored Women . . . 1897*.

60. Subject Files, National Association of Colored Women, 1897–1962, Mary Church Terrell Papers, Manuscript Division, Library of Congress, Washington, D.C.

61. Mary Church Terrell Papers, Manuscript Department, Moorland-Spingarn Research Center, Howard University, Washington, D.C.

62. Ibid. See also Addie Hunton, "Negro Womanhood Defended," *Voice of the Negro* 1 (July 1904): 280–82, writes, "Any argument that does not take more than passing note of the heritage of shame with which she found herself burdened when emerging from slavery, or that does not take more than a mere glance at her very peculiar environment, is at best but erroneous."

63. Wesley, *The History of the National Association*, 45, 46.

64. Josephine Silone Yates, "Kindergartens and Mothers' Clubs as Related to the Work of the National Association of Colored Women," *Colored American Magazine* (1905): 305.

65. A. H. Hunton, "Kindergarten Work in the South," *Alexander's Magazine* 2, no. 3 (July 1906): 29–32.

## 5. What Do Nineteenth-Century Reformers Have to Say to Twentieth-Century Liberationists?

1. "The Woman's Mutual Improvement Club," *Woman's Era*, February 1895, 15.

2. Hamilton, "The National Association of Colored Women," 78, suggests that because work done by club women had previously been undertaken in auxiliaries of the black church, the club movement denoted a shift in a "power relationship." With this shift, she writes, "A slow, almost imperceptible change occurred which resulted in Black women

having more control over how they would use their energies on behalf of the race." This is yet another earmark of how the club movement was a movement against gender oppression.

3. Linda Perkins, "Black Women and Racial 'Uplift' Prior to Emancipation," *The Black Woman Cross-Culturally*, ed. Filomina Chioma Steady (Cambridge, Mass.: Schenkman, 1981), 317–34. Higginbotham, *Righteous Discontent*, 194–204, notes that "uplift" signifies "assimilationist leanings" because it was linked to a "politics of respectability."

4. Hamilton, "The National Association of Colored Women," 79–80, notes, "Women of comparative wealth and education were undoubtedly responsible for much of the activity surrounding the regional and national conferences since this required not only money but a vast amount of planning skill. But the hundreds of organizations which made the national network possible were composed of average women. Sharecropping housewives, students, salesgirls and dressmakers were involved as well as artists, teachers, and school principals."

5. For discussions that describe a certain elitism on the part of club leaders, see Davis, *Women, Race, and Class*, 134; Lerner, "Early Community Work of Club Women," 160; and Moses, *The Golden Age of Black Nationalism*, chapter 5.

6. Hamilton, "The National Association of Colored Women," 135.

7. Mary Church Terrell, "What Role Is the Educated Negro Woman to Play in the Uplifting of Her Race?" *Twentieth Century Negro Literature: A Cyclopedia of Thought on the Vital Topics Relating to the American Negro*, ed. D. W. Culp (Naperville, Ill.: J. L. Nichols, 1902; reprinted, New York: Arno Press, New York Times, 1969), 176–77.

8. H. Richard Niebuhr, *The Responsible Self* (New York: Harper and Row, 1963), 60–61, and "The Center of Value," *Radical Monotheism and Western Culture* (New York: Harper and Row, 1960), 100–113. Niebuhr's ethic of responsibility has been described as one that seeks to (1) address the problem of "the polytheism of multiple value centers in the name of monotheism" and (2) develop responsibility as a normative principle in terms of "rules (first principles) for responsible response" whereby value is apprehended "in the experience of actual and potential interrelationships." It is in these two ways primarily that Niebuhr's ethic is an appropriate model and dialogue partner for this discussion of club women's thought as an ethic of responsibility. Also, for a full-fledged explication and extension of the Niebuhrian responsibilist tradition through a dialogue with African American moral exemplars of the nineteenth century, see Darryl M. Trimiew, *Voices of the Silenced: The Responsible Self in a Marginalized Community* (Cleveland: The Pilgrim Press, 1993).

9. See Niebuhr, *The Responsible Self*, 61–65, for a discussion of re-

sponse, interpretation, accountability, and social solidarity as elements of a theory of responsibility.

10. See Niebuhr, "The Center of Value," 112–13.

11. See Niebuhr, *The Responsible Self*, 87–88, 118, 119, 126, for a discussion of responsibility in universal context and absolute dependence as well as the way club women's position seems consistent with this summary statement of Niebuhr's ethic: "Responsibility affirms: God is acting in all actions upon you. so respond to all actions upon you as to respond to his action."

12. It is at this point that the club women's understanding qualifies the Niebuhrian ethic. Their ethic insists that the responsible self is a sociohistorical being even as God creates her or him. It seems to me that Niebuhr's social self lapses into an ahistorical ethical posture whereas the club women's does not. This is the case, if I am reading Trimiew correctly in *Voices of the Silenced*, because Niebuhr's social self is an "empowered" self rather than a "marginalized" self. Trimiew suggests that marginalized responsible selves extend Niebuhr's tradition because they understand appropriate response to God and others as meeting basic human needs coupled with the recognition of basic human rights. See especially, Trimiew, *Voices of the Silenced*, xii–xvii, 8–19, chapter 5.

13. See my essay, "The Logic of Interstructured Oppression: A Black Womanist Perspective," *Redefining Sexual Ethics* (Cleveland: The Pilgrim Press, 1991), where I develop the concept of relationality and this logic with reference to relationships between black women and white women as members of sociohistorical groups.

14. This typification of black religious liberation and womanist thought seeks to capture representative understandings in the works of authors including, but not limited to, James Cone, J. Deotis Roberts, Major Jones, Enoch Oglesby, Katie G. Cannon, and Delores S. Williams. My remarks are informed by the discussion of the limited formal ethical understandings within black liberation theology as articulated by Peter Paris in "The Task of Religious Social Ethics in Light of Black Theology," *Liberation and Ethics*, ed. Charles Amjad-Ali and W. Alvin Pitcher (Chicago: Center for the Scientific Study of Religion, 1985), 135–43.

15. C. Eric Lincoln, *Race, Religion and the Continuing American Dilemma* (New York: Hill and Wang, 1984), 223–27. Compare "Roots III: Souls on Ice: A Post Civil Rights Generation Struggles for Identity," *Newsweek*, 10 June 1985, 82–84. The subject of this article is a deracination process that often affects children of upwardly mobile Blacks.

16. I would interpret many of the comments made by members of the black middle class in Ellis Cose's *Rage of a Privileged Class* (New York: HarperCollins, 1993) to be illustrative of this point.

17. James Cone, *For My People: Black Theology and the Black Church* (Maryknoll, N.Y.: Orbis Books, 1984), 193.

18. See, for example, "Middle-Class Blacks Try to Grip a Ladder While Lending a Hand," *New York Times*, 26 November 1990.

19. See Sharon M. Collins, "The Making of the Black Middle Class," *Social Problems* 30 (April 1983): 380.

20. I distinguish my position from those of black neoconservatives who place an overwhelming emphasis upon valuational change among black people and strident black separatists who espouse the need to remain completely apart from the larger society as key to black liberation. Instead, I suggest that the needed socioethical stance among black people is one that takes seriously aspects of each of those two positions. Black people must not be afraid to name the negative values that we have assimilated nor should we relinquish our separate black institutions because our goal has been integration. We must face some hard facts about ourselves and our condition: our present value systems are not strong enough to sustain us in the midst of an anger and hatred derived from the reality that we will never be integrated into U.S. society and that we are dying either at the hands of one another or from the despair we feel. Facing this, we can become authentically creative again— nurturing values for a liberative moral agency and vision that does not deny our past attempts at integration or separatism but which is filled with a present hope for inclusion on terms that require neither assimilation of a single normative "white" standard for humanity nor separation out of bitter resentment.

## 6. Socioreligious Moral Vision for the Twenty-first Century

1. This discussion of embodiment is informed generally by feminists' reclamation of the body and particularly by the systematic appropriation of that understanding by authors such as James Nelson, *Embodiment: An Approach to Sexuality and Christian Theology* (Minneapolis: Augsburg, 1978). Also Rebecca J. Kruger Gaudino, "Black Women and the Embodied Experience of Intimate Health Care: A Christian White Woman's Learnings and Wonderings" (unpublished paper), captures this understanding of the relationship between createdness and embodiment when she writes, "But theologians have carefully avoided the statement that human embodiment itself—the manifestation of God's creation—is in the image of God: God is a spirit, it is stated, and cannot be understood in terms of embodiment. But this reading, it seems to me, refuses to take the Genesis assertion seriously—that we in our particular createdness, our embodied femaleness and maleness, reflect the very likeness of God.

If we entertain the notion that our very physicality communicates, however mysteriously, something about the life of God, it is possible to reclaim a large portion of human reality too long ignored and devalued as in no way reflecting God," 74.

2. *A History of the Club Movement*, 5.

3. From an address by Mary Church Terrell in the Mary Church Terrell Papers, Manuscript Department, Moorland-Spingarn Research Center, Howard University, Washington, D.C.

4. Niebuhr, *The Responsible Self*, 57–58, 60–61.

5. *Minutes of the National Association of Colored Women*, 12.

### 7. A Sermonic Fragment

1. Colleagues at Columbia Seminary have noted that the elements of the club women's moral vision brought the biblical texts of Philippians 2:1–8 and Galatians 3:23–29 to mind as meaningful points for engaging in a mediating ethical process between the women's insights and biblical texts. Such engagement with biblical texts is an important part of contemporary Christian ethical reflection as mediating process. I intend to provide more precise guidance for this type of ethical reflection in a future book wherein I rethink the discipline of Christian ethics from a womanist perspective.

# Selected Bibliography

## General

Alexander, William T. *History of the Colored Race in America*. Kansas City: Palmette, 1887; reprinted, New York: Negro Universities Press, 1968.

Allen, Robert L. *Black Awakening in Capitalist America*. New York: Doubleday Anchor Books, 1970.

Allen, Robert L., and Pamela P. Allen. *Reluctant Reformers: Racism and Social Reform Movements in the United States*. Washington, D.C.: Howard University Press, 1974.

Aptheker, Herbert, ed. *A Documentary History of the Negro People in the U.S.*, preface by W. E. B. DuBois. New York: Citadel Press, 1951.

Baker, Ray Stannard. *Following the Color Line: American Negro Citizenship in the Progressive Era*. 1908. Reprint, New York: Doubleday, Page, 1964.

Barber, Bernard. *Social Stratification: A Comparative Analysis of Structure and Process*. New York: Harcourt, Brace, 1957.

Bendix, Richard, and Seymour Lipset, eds. *Class, Status, and Power*. Glencoe, Ill.: Free Press, 1953.

Bennett, Lerone. *Before the Mayflower*. 5th ed. Chicago: Johnson Publishing, 1984.

―――. *Black Power, U.S.A.: The Human Side of Reconstruction, 1867–1877*. Chicago: Johnson Publishing, 1967.

―――. "Liberation." *Ebony* 25 (1970): 36–45.

―――. "No Crystal Stair: The Black Woman in History." *Ebony* 2 (August 1977): 164–170.

―――. *Pioneers in Protest*. Baltimore: Penguin Books, 1969.

―――. *The Shaping of Black America*. Chicago: Johnson Publishing Co., 1975.

Berlin, Ira. *Slaves Without Masters: The Free Negro in the Antebellum South*. New York: Pantheon Books, 1974.

Berry, Mary F., and John W. Blassingame. *Long Memory: The Black Experience in America*. New York: Oxford University Press, 1982.

Blackwell, James. *The Black Community: Diversity and Unity*. 2d ed. New York: Harper and Row, 1985.

Blackwell, James, and Morris Janowitz. *Black Sociologists: Historical and Contemporary Perspectives*. Chicago: University of Chicago Press, 1974.

Blassingame, John W. *Black New Orleans: 1860–1880*. Chicago: University of Chicago Press, 1973.

———. "The Revolution That Never Was: The Civil Rights Movement, 1950–1980." *Perspectives: The Civil Rights Quarterly* 14:2 (summer 1982): 3–15.

———. *The Slave Community: Plantation Life in the Antebellum South*. 2d ed. New York: Oxford University Press, 1979.

———. "Status and Social Structure in the Slave Community," *The Afro-American Slaves: Community or Chaos*, edited by Randall M. Miller. Malabar, Fla.: Robert E. Kreiger, 1981.

Blauner, Robert. "Black Culture: Myth or Reality," *Afro-American Anthropology*, edited by Norman Whitten and John Swed. New York: Doubleday, 1970.

———. "Internal Colonialism and Ghetto Revolt." *Social Problems* 16 (spring 1969): 393–408.

———. *Racial Oppression in America*. New York: Harper and Row, 1972.

Bloom, Jack M. *Class, Race, and the Civil Rights Movement*. Bloomington: Indiana University Press, 1987.

Boxill, Bernard R. *Blacks and Social Justice*. Totowa, N.J.: Rowman and Allanheld, 1984.

Brawley, Benjamin. *A Social History of the American Negro*. New York: AMS Press, 1971.

Brisbane, Robert. *Black Activism: Racial Revolution in the U.S., 1954–1970*. Valley Forge, Pa.: Judson Press, 1974.

———. *The Black Vanguard*. Valley Forge, Pa.: Judson Press, 1970.

Brittan, Arthur, and Mary Maynard. *Sexism, Racism and Oppression*. New York: Blackwell, 1984.

Browne, Robert S. "Black Economic Autonomy." *Black Scholar*, October 1971, 26–31.

Bryce, Herrington J. "Are Most Blacks in the Middle Class?" *Black Scholar* 5 (February 1974): 32–36.

Bureau of the Census. *The Social and Economic Status of the Black Population in the United States: An Historical View, 1790–1978*. Washington, D.C.: Government Printing Office, 1980.

Camejo, Peter. *Racism, Revolution, Reaction, 1861–1877: The Rise and Fall of Radical Reconstruction*. New York: Pathfinder Press, 1976.

Cayton, Horace M., and St. Clair Drake. *Black Metropolis: A Study of Negro Life in a Northern City*. 1945. Reprint, New York: Harper and Row, 1962.

Clark, Kenneth. *Dark Ghetto*. New York: Harper and Row, 1965.

Collins, Randall. *Conflict Sociology: Toward an Explanatory Science*. New York: Academic Press, 1975.

Collins, Sharon M. "The Making of the Black Middle Class." *Social Problems* 30, no. 4 (April 1983): 369–82.

Conti, Joseph G., and Brad Stetson. *Challenging the Civil Rights Establishment: Profiles of a New Black Vanguard*. Westport, Conn.: Praeger, 1993.

Cose, Ellis. *The Rage of a Privileged Class*. New York: Harper Collins, 1993.

Cox, Oliver Cromwell. *Caste, Class, and Race*. Garden City, N.Y.: Doubleday, 1948.

Cross, Theodore. *Black Capitalism*. New York: Atheneum, 1969.

Cruse, Harold. *The Crisis of the Negro Intellectual*. New York: William Morrow, 1967.

Cone, James H. "Black Consciousness and the Black Church: A Historical-Theological Interpretation," *Religion's Influence in Contemporary Society*, edited by Joseph E. Faulkner. Columbus, Ohio: Charles E. Merrill, 1972.

———. *For My People: Black Theology and the Black Church*. Maryknoll, N.Y.: Orbis Books, 1984.

———. *God of the Oppressed*. New York: Seabury Press, 1975.

Curry, Leonard P. *The Free Black in Urban America, 1800–1850: The Shadow of the Dream*. Chicago: University of Chicago Press, 1981.

Davis, Allison, B. Burleigh, and Mary R. Gardner. *Deep South*. Washington, D.C.: American Council on Education, 1940.

Davis, John P. *The American Negro Reference Book*. Englewood Cliffs, N.J.: Prentice-Hall, 1966.

Davis, Kingsley, and Wilbert E. Moore. "Some Principles of Stratification." *American Sociological Review* 10 (1945): 242–49.

Daniel, Johnnie. "Negro Political Behavior and Community Political and Socio-Economic Structural Factors." *Social Forces* 47 (March 1969).

Daniels, Lee A. "The New Black Conservative." *New York Times*, 4 October 1981, 20.

Deats, Paul, ed. *Toward a Discipline of Social Ethics: Essays in Honor of Walter George Muedler*. Boston: Boston University Press, 1972.

Dill, Bonnie Thornton. "The Dialectics of Black Womanhood." *Signs* 4 (spring 1979).

Drake, St. Clair. *Black Metropolis: A Study of Negro Life in a Northern City*. New York: Harcourt, Brace, and Company, 1945.

———. "The Social and Economic Status of the Negro in the United

States," *The Negro American*, edited by Talcott Parsons and Kenneth B. Clark. Boston: Beacon Press, 1967.

Draper, Theodore. *The Rediscovery of Black Nationalism*. New York: Viking, 1970.

DuBois, W. E. B. *Black Folk Then and Now: An Essay in the History and Sociology of the Negro Race*. New York: H. Holt, 1939.

————. *The Black North in 1901: A Social Study*. New York: Arno Press, 1969.

————. *Black Reconstruction*. New York: Harcourt, Brace, 1935.

————. *Darkwater: Voices from Within the Veil*. 1920. Reprint, Millwood, N.Y.: Kraus-Thomson, 1975.

————. *The Negro*. New York: H. Holt, 1915.

————. *The Negro American Family*. Atlanta: Atlanta University Press, 1908.

————. *The Negro Artisan*. Atlanta: Atlanta University Press, 1902.

————. *The Philadelphia Negro*. Philadelphia: University of Pennsylvania, 1899.

————. *The Souls of Black Folk*. 1903. Reprint, Millwood, N.Y.: Kraus-Thomson, 1973.

————, ed. *Manners and Morals*. Atlanta: Atlanta University Press, 1900.

————, ed. *Some Efforts of American Negroes for Their Own Betterment*. Atlanta: Atlanta University Press, 1898.

DuBois, W. E. B., and Booker T. Washington. *The Negro in the South: His Economic Progress in Relation to His Moral and Religious Development*. 1907. Reprint, New York: Citadel Press, 1970.

Edwards, G. Franklin. "Community and Class Relations: The Ordeal of Change," *The Negro American*, edited by Talcott Parsons and Kenneth B. Clark. Boston: Beacon Press, 1967.

Edwards, Herbert O. "Black Theology and the Black Revolution." *Union Seminary Quarterly Review* 31 (fall 1975).

————. "Towards a Black Christian Social Ethic," *Duke Divinity School Review* 40 (spring 1975).

Essien-Udom, E. U. *Black Nationalism*. 1964. Reprint, Chicago: University of Chicago Press, 1971.

Evans, James H. "Black Theology and Black Feminism." *Journal of Religious Thought* 38 (spring-summer 1981).

Farley, Reynolds. *Blacks and Whites: Narrowing the Gap?* Cambridge, Mass.: Harvard University Press, 1984.

Farley, Reynolds, and Walter R. Allen. *The Color Line and the Quality of Life in America*. New York: Russell Sage Foundation, 1987.

Franklin, John Hope. *From Slavery to Freedom*. 6th ed. New York: Knopf, 1988.

————. *Reconstruction: After the Civil War*. Chicago: University of Chicago Press, 1961.

Frazier, E. Franklin. *Black Bourgeoisie*. New York: Collier Books, 1962.
————. "Ethnic Family Patterns: The Negro Family in the United States." *American Journal of Sociology* 53 (May 1948): 435–38.
————. *The Negro in the U.S.* New York: The Macmillan Co., 1949.
————. *The Negro Church in America*. New York: Schocken Books, 1964.
————. *The Negro Family in the U.S.* Rev. and abridged ed. New York: Dryden Press, 1948.
Freeman, Richard. *The Black Elite*. New York: McGraw-Hill, 1976.
Genovese, Eugene. *Roll, Jordan, Roll: The World the Slaves Made*. New York: Pantheon Books, 1974.
Ginzberg, Eli. *The Middle Class Negro in the White Man's World*. New York: Columbia University Press, 1967.
Glasgow, Douglas G. *The Black Underclass: Poverty, Unemployment and the Entrapment of Ghetto Youth*. New York: Vintage, 1981.
Grier, William, and Price Cobb. *Black Rage*. New York: Basic Books, 1968.
Grunlan, Stephen A., and Milton Reimer, eds. *Christian Perspectives on Sociology*. Grand Rapids, Mich.: Zondervan, 1982.
Hamilton, Charles V., and Stokely Carmichael. *Black Power: The Politics of Liberation in America*. New York: Random House, 1967.
Harding, Vincent. *There Is a River: The Black Struggle for Freedom in America*. New York: Harcourt Brace Jovanovich, 1981.
Hare, Nathan. *Black Anglo-Saxons*. London: Macmillan, 1970.
Harris, George B. "Boston Colored People." *Colored American Magazine* 14, no. 1 (January 1908): 29–31.
Harris, William H. *The Harder We Run: Black Workers Since the Civil War*. New York: Oxford University Press, 1982.
Harrison, Beverly. "Theological Reflection in the Struggle for Liberation," *Making the Connections*, edited by Carol S. Robb. Boston: Beacon Press, 1985.
Hawks, Joan V., and Sheila L. Skemp, eds. *Sex, Race, and the Role of Women in the South*. Jackson: University of Mississippi Press, 1983.
Henri, Florette. *Black Migration: Movement North, 1900–1920*. New York: Anchor Press, 1975.
Higgins, Nathan et al., eds. *Key Issues in the Afro-American Experience*. New York: Harcourt Brace Jovanovich, 1971.
Hine, Darlene Clark, ed. *The State of Afro-American History: Past, Present, Future*. Baton Rouge: Louisiana State University Press, 1986.
Hyman, Herbert. "The Value Systems of Different Classes: A Social Psychology Contribution to the Analysis of Stratification," *Class Status and Power: A Reader in Social Stratification*. New York: Free Press, 1953.
Jacobs, John E., ed. *The State of Black America 1983–1988*. New York: National Urban League, 1983.
Janeway, Elizabeth. *Man's World, Woman's Place: A Study in Social Mytho-*

*logy*. New York: William Morrow, 1971.

Johnson, Charles S. *Growing Up in the Black Belt*. Washington, D.C.: American Council on Education, 1941.

———. *Shadow of the Plantation*. Chicago: University of Chicago Press, 1934.

Jonsen, Albert R. *Responsibility in Modern Religious Ethics*. Washington, D.C.: Corpus Books, 1968.

Katzman, David M. *Before the Ghetto: Black Detroit in the 19th Century*. Urbana: University of Illinois Press, 1973.

Kletzing, H. F., and W. H. Crogman. *Progress of a Race or the Remarkable Advance of the Afro-American*. Atlanta: J. L. Nichols, 1897.

Kronus, Sidney. *The Black Middle Class*. Columbus, Ohio: Charles E. Merrill, 1971.

———. "Some Neglected Areas of Negro Class Comparisons," *Race Relations*, edited by Edgar G. Epps. Cambridge, Mass.: Winthrop, 1973.

Ladner, Joyce A., ed. *The Death of White Sociology*. New York: Random House, 1973.

Landry, Bart. *The New Black Middle Class*. Berkeley: University of California Press, 1987.

Leventman, Seymour. "Class and Ethnic Tensions: Minority Group Leadership in Transition." *Sociology and Social Research* 50 (April 1966).

Levitan, Sar A., William B. Johnson, and Robert Taggart. *Still a Dream: The Changing Status of Blacks Since 1960*. Cambridge, Mass.: Harvard University Press, 1975.

Lieberson, Stanley. *A Piece of the Pie: Blacks and White Immigrants Since 1880*. Berkeley: University of California Press, 1980.

Lincoln, C. Eric. *Race, Religion, and the Continuing American Dilemma*. New York: Hill and Wang, 1984.

Logan, Rayford W. *The Betrayal of the Negro, from Rutherford B. Hayes to Woodrow Wilson*. New York: Collier Books, 1965.

Lourde, Audre. *Sister Outsider: Essays and Speeches*. New York: Crossing Press, 1984.

Lynch, Hollis. *The Black Urban Condition*. New York: Thomas Y. Crowell, 1973.

Marable, Manning. "Beyond the Race-Class Dilemma." *Nation*, 11 April 1981, 417–36.

———. "Black Conservatives and Accommodation: Of Thomas Sowell and Others." *Negro History Bulletin* 45 (April-June 1982): 32–35.

———. *Blackwater: Historical Studies in Race, Class Consciousness, and Revolution*. Dayton, Ohio: Black Praxis Press, 1981.

———. "The Crisis of the Black Working Class: An Economic and Historical Analysis." *Science and Society* 46 (summer 1982): 130–61.

———. *From the Grassroots: Social and Political Essays Towards Afro-American Liberation.* Boston: South End Press, 1980.

———. *How Capitalism Underdeveloped Black America.* Boston: South End Press, 1983.

———. *Race, Reform, and Rebellion: The Second Reconstruction in Black America.* Jackson: University of Mississippi, 1984.

———. "Reaganism, Racism, and Reaction: Black Political Realignment in the 1980s." *The Black Scholar* 13, no. 6 (fall 1982): 2–15.

Masuoka, Jitsuichi, and Preston Valien, eds. *Race Relations: Problems and Theory.* Chapel Hill: University of North Carolina Press, 1961.

Meier, August. "Negro Class Structure and Ideology in the Age of Booker T. Washington." *Phylon* 23:3 (1962): 258–66.

———. *Negro Thought in America: 1880–1915.* Ann Arbor: University of Michigan Press, 1966.

Meier, August, John H. Bracey, Jr., and Elliot Rudwick, eds. *Black Matriarchy: Myth or Reality?* Belmont: Wadsworth, 1971.

Meier, August, and Elliot Rudwick. *From Plantation to Ghetto.* New York: Hill and Wang, 1976.

———. *The Making of Black America: Essays in Negro Life and History.* New York: Atheneum, 1969.

Miller, Kelly. *Radicals and Conservatives: And Other Essays on the Negro in America.* 1908. Reprint, New York: Schocken, 1968.

Mitchell, Mozella G. "The Black Woman's View of Human Liberation." *Theology Today* 39 (January 1983).

Morris, Richard T., and Raymond J. Murphy. "A Paradigm for the Study of Class Consciousness." *Sociology and Social Research* 50 (April 1966).

Muelder, Walter G. *Moral Law in Christian Social Ethics.* Richmond: John Knox, 1966.

Myrdal, Gunner. *An American Dilemma.* New York: Harper and Row, 1944.

*New York Times Magazine.* "The Black Plight, Race or Class?" 27 June 1980.

Niebuhr, H. Richard. "The Center of Value," *Radical Monotheism and Western Culture.* New York: Harper Torchbooks, 1970.

———. *The Responsible Self.* New York: Harper and Row, 1963.

Ofari, Earl. *The Myth of Black Capitalism.* New York: Atlantic Monthly Press, 1970.

Oglesby, Enoch. *Ethics and Theology from the Other Side: Sounds of Moral Struggles.* Washington, D.C.: University Press of America, 1979.

Paris, Peter. *The Social Teaching of the Black Churches.* Philadelphia: Fortress Press, 1985.

———. "The Task of Religious Social Ethics in Light of Black Theology,"

*Liberation and Ethics,* edited by Charles Amjad-Ali and W. Alvin Pitcher. Chicago: Center for the Scientific Study of Religion, 1985.

Pinkney, Alphonso. *Black Americans.* 2d ed. Englewood Cliffs: Prentice-Hall, 1969.

———. *The Myth of Black Progress.* New York: Cambridge University Press, 1984.

Pollard, William L. *A Study of Black Self-Help.* San Francisco: R and E Research Associates, 1978.

Poxpey, C. Spencer. "The Washington-DuBois Controversy and Its Effect on the Negro Problem." *History of Education Journal* 8, no. 4 (1957): 128–52.

Quarles, Benjamin. *The Negro in the Making of America.* Rev. ed. New York: Collier Books, 1969.

Rabinowitz, Howard N. *Race Relations in the Urban South, 1865–1890.* New York: Oxford University Press, 1978.

Rainwater, Lee. "Crucible of Identity: The Negro Lower-Class Family," *The Negro American,* edited by Talcott Parsons and Kenneth B. Clark. Boston: Beacon Press, 1967.

Richardson, Joe M. *Christian Reconstruction: The American Missionary Association and Southern Blacks, 1861–1890.* Athens: University of Georgia Press, 1986.

Riley, Norman. "Attitudes of the Black Middle Class." *Crisis,* December 1986.

Roberts, J. Deotis. *A Black Political Theology.* Philadelphia: Westminster Press, 1974.

———. *Liberation and Reconciliation: A Black Theology.* Philadelphia: Westminster Press, 1973.

Roof, Wade Clark, and Daphne Spain. "A Research Note on City-Suburban Socio-economic Differences Among Blacks." *Social Forces* 56 (September 1977): 15–20.

Rule, Shelia. "Black Middle Class Slipping, Study by Urban League Says." *New York Times,* 4 August 1982.

Ryan, William. *Blaming the Victim.* New York: Vintage Brooks, 1971.

Sampson, William. A. "New Insights on Black Middle-Class Mobility." *Urban League Review* 5, no. 1 (summer 1980): 21–24.

Schaefer, Richard T. *Racial and Ethnic Groups.* Boston: Little, Brown, 1979.

Schuman, Howard, Charlotte Steech, and Lawrence Bobo. *Racial Attitudes in America: Trends and Interpretations.* Cambridge, Mass.: Harvard University Press, 1985.

Sennett, Richard, and Jonathan Cobb. *The Hidden Injuries of Class.* New York: Vintage Books, 1973.

Shaw, Talbert O. "Responsibility and Middle Class Religion." Ph.D. diss., University of Chicago, 1973.

Smith, Archie. *The Relational Self: Ethics and Therapy from a Black Church Perspective*. Nashville: Abingdon, 1982.

Smith, Charles U. "The Black Middle Class and the Struggle for Civil Rights," *Black America*. New York: Basic Books, 1970.

Smythe, Mayble M., ed. *The Black American Reference*. Englewood Cliffs, N.J.: Prentice-Hall, 1976.

Stampp, Kenneth. *The Peculiar Institution: Slavery in the AnteBellum South*. New York: Knopf, 1958.

Staples, Robert. *Introduction to Black Sociology*. New York: McGraw-Hill, 1976.

Steinberg, Stephen. *The Ethnic Myth: Race, Ethnicity, and Class in America*. Boston: Beacon Press, 1981.

Stuckey, Sterling. *Slave Culture: Nationalist Theory and the Foundations of Black America*. New York: Oxford University Press, 1987.

Takaki, Ronald T. *Iron Cages: Race and Culture in 19th-Century America*. New York: Knopf, 1979.

Toll, William. *The Resurgence of Race: Black Social Theory from Reconstruction to the Pan African Conferences*. Philadelphia: Temple University Press, 1979.

Trimiew, Darryl M. *Voices of the Silenced: The Responsible Self in a Marginalized Community*. Cleveland: The Pilgrim Press, 1993.

Tumin, Melvin M., ed. *Readings on Social Stratification*. Englewood Cliffs, N.J.: Prentice-Hall, 1970.

Vanfossen, Beth E. *The Structure of Social Inequality*. Boston: Little, Brown, 1979.

Vanneman, Reeve, and Lynn Weber Cannon. *The American Perception of Class*. Philadelphia: Temple University Press, 1987.

Walker, Alice. *In Search of Our Mothers' Gardens: Womanist Prose*. San Diego: Harcourt Brace Jovanovich, 1983.

Wallace, Michelle. *Black Macho and the Myth of the Superwoman*. New York: Warner Books, 1979.

Ward, Dawn McNeal. "Social Stratification: Social Class and Social Mobility," *Christian Perspectives of Sociology*, edited by Stephen A. Grunlan and Milton Reimer. Grand Rapids, Mich.: Zondervan, 1982.

Washington, Booker T. *The Future of the American Negro*. Boston: Small, Maynard, 1899.

———. *A New Negro for a New Century*. New York: Arno Press, 1969.

———. *The Story of the Negro: The Rise of the Race from Slavery*. New York: Doubleday, Page, 1909.

Washington, Joseph R. *Dilemmas of the New Black Middle Class*. Philadelphia: University of Pennsylvania Press, 1980.

West, Cornel. *Prophesy Deliverance!* Philadelphia: Westminster Press, 1982.

————. *Race Matters*. Boston: Beacon Press, 1993.

————. "Unmasking the Black Conservatives." *Christian Century*, 16–23 July 1986.

Williams, George Washington. *History of the Negro Race in America, 1619–1880*. New York: Arno Press, New York Times, 1968.

Williams, Loretta. "Race and Class in the Eighties: Disentangling a Double Bind." *Christianity and Crisis*, 30 March 1981.

Williams, Preston M. "Criteria for Decision-Making for Social Ethics in the Black Community." *Journal of the Interdenominational Theological Center*, fall 1973.

Willie, Charles V., ed. *The Caste and Class Controversy*. Bayside, N.Y.: General Hall, 1979.

Wilson, William J. *The Declining Significance of Race: Blacks and Changing American Institutions*. 1979. 2d ed., Chicago: University of Chicago Press, 1980.

————. "The Declining Significance of Race: Revisited but Not Revised," *Caste and Class Controversy*, edited by Charles Vert Willie. Bayside: General Hall, 1979.

————. *The Truly Disadvantaged: The Inner City, the Underclass, and Public Policy*. Chicago: University of Chicago Press, 1987.

Winston, Henry. *Class, Race, and Black Liberation*. New York: International Publishers, 1977.

## Works by or on Nineteenth-Century Women

Addams, Jane, and Ida B. Wells. *Lynching and Rape: An Exchange of Views*, edited by Bettina Apetheker. New York: American Institute for Marxist Studies, 1977, 1982.

Andolsen, Barbara. *"Daughters of Jefferson, Daughters of Bootblacks": Racism and American Feminism*. Macon: Mercer University Press, 1986.

Andrews, William L., ed. *Sisters of the Spirit: Three Black Women's Autobiographies of the 19th Century*. Bloomington: Indiana University Press, 1986.

Aptheker, Bettina. *Women's Legacy: Essays on Race, Sex, and Class in American History*. Amherst: University of Massachusetts Press, 1982.

Barnette, Evelyn Brooks. "Nannie Burroughs and the Education of Black Women," *The Afro-American Woman: Struggles and Images*, edited by Sharon Harley and Rosalyn Terborg-Penn. Port Washington, N.Y.: Kennikat Press, 1978.

Bennett, Lerone. "The Negro Woman." *Ebony*, August 1960.

————. "No Crystal Stair: The Black Woman in History." *Ebony* 32 (August 1977): 164–70.

Blauvelt, Mary Taylor. "The Race Problem: As Discussed by Negro Women." *American Journal of Sociology* 6 (March 1901): 662–72.

Bogin, Ruth, and Bert James Loewenberg, eds. *Black Women in Nineteenth Century American Life: Their Words, Their Thoughts, Their Feelings.* University Park: Pennsylvania State University Press, 1976.

Bowser, R. "What Role Is the Educated Negro Woman to Play in the Uplifting of Her Race?" *Twentieth-Century Negro Literature: Or a Cyclopedia of Thought on the Vital Topics Relating to American Negro,* edited by D. Culp. Toronto: J. L. Nichols, 1902.

Brawley, Benjamin G. *Women of Achievement.* Chicago: Women's American Baptist Home Mission Society, 1919.

Brown, Hallie Quinn. *Homespun Heroines and Other Women of Distinction.* 1926. Reprint, Freeport, N.Y.: Books for Libraries Press, 1971.

Brown, Jean Collier. "The Economic Status of Negro Women." *Southern Workman* 60 (October 1931): 430–31.

Bruce, Josephine. "What Has Education Done for Colored Women." *Voice of the Negro* 1 (July 1904): 294–98.

Burroughs, Nannie. "Black Women and Reform." *Crisis* 10 (1915): 187.

———. "A Clarion Call to Duty." *Colored American* 5 (April 1905): 2.

———. "The Colored Woman and Her Relationship to the Domestic Problem," *The United Negro,* edited by J. W. E. Bowen. Atlanta: D. E. Luther Publishing, 1902.

———. "Not Color but Character." *Voice of the Negro* 1 (July 1904): 277–79.

Cade, Toni. *The Black Woman: An Anthology.* New York: Signet, 1970.

Cash, Floris Loretta Barnett. "Womanhood and Protest: The Club Movement Among Black Women, 1892–1922." Ph.D. diss., State University of New York at Stony Brook, 1986.

Cannon, Katie Geneva. *Black Womanist Ethics.* Atlanta: Scholars Press, 1988.

———. "The Emergence of Black Feminist Consciousness," *Feminist Interpretation of the Bible,* edited by Letty M. Russell. Philadelphia: Westminster Press, 1985.

———. "Resources for a Constructive Ethic in the Life and Work of Zora Neale Hurston." *Journal of Feminist Studies in Religion* 1 (spring 1985).

Cheagle, Rosalyn. "The Colored Temperance Movement: 1830–1860." M.A. thesis, Howard University, 1969.

Clinton, Catherine. *The Other Civil War: American Women in the Nineteenth Century.* New York: Hill and Wang, 1984.

Cole, Johnetta. "Black Women in America: An Annotated Bibliography." *Black Scholar,* December 1971, 42–53.

Coleman, Willie Mae. "Keeping the Faith and Disturbing the Peace: Black Woman from Anti-Slavery to Women's Suffrage." Ph.D. diss., University of California, Irvine, 1982.

Conway, Jill K., ed. "Women's Clubs," *The Female Experience in the 18th and 19th Century America.* New York: Garland, 1982.

Cooper, Anna J. "The Ethics of the Negro." Unpublished Paper, September 1902. Anna J. Cooper Papers. Moorland-Spingarn Research Center, Howard University.

————. "The Third Step." Anna Julia Cooper Papers. Moorland-Spingarn Research Center, Howard University.

————. *A Voice from the South: By a Black Woman of the South.* Xenia, Oh.: Aldine Printing House, 1892.

"National Federation of Women's Clubs." *Crisis,* June 1920, 100.

Crummell, Alexander. *The Black Woman of the South: Her Neglects and Her Needs.* Washington, D.C.: Alexander Crummell, 1881.

Davis, Angela. *Women, Race, and Class.* New York: Random House, 1981.

Davis, Elizabeth. *Lifting As They Climb: The National Association of Colored Women.* Washington, D.C.: National Association of Colored Women, 1933.

Davis, John P., ed. *The American Negro Reference Book.* Englewood Cliffs, N.J.: Prentice-Hall, 1966.

Desselle, Francis A. "The Life and Contributions of Mary Church Terrell." M.A. thesis, Howard University School of Education, 1974.

Duster, Alfreda, ed. *Crusade for Justice: The Autobiography of Ida B. Wells.* Chicago: University of Chicago Press, 1972.

Eugene, Toinette. "While Love Is Unfashionable," *Women's Consciousness, Women's Conscience.* New York: Winston Press, 1985.

————. "Moral Values and Black Womanists." *Journal of Religious Thought* 41, no. 2 (1984–85).

"First National Conference of Colored Women, Held July 29, 30, 31, 1895 at Boston." *Women's Era* 5 (1895): 14.

Flexner, Eleanor. *Century of Struggle: The Women's Rights Movement in the U.S.* Cambridge, Mass.: Harvard University Press, 1959.

Genoese, Eugene. "The Negro Woman." *Masses and Mainstream* 2 (February 1949): 10–17.

————. "The Slave Family: Women—A Reassessment of Matriarchy, Emasculation, Weakness." *Southern Voices,* August-September 1974, 9–16.

Gibson, J. W., and W. H. Crogman. *Progress of a Race, Or the Remarkable Advancement of the Colored American.* Naperville, Ill.: J. L. Nichols, 1902, 1912.

Giddings, Paula. *When and Where I Enter.* New York: William Morrow, 1984.

Gifford, Carolyn de Swarte. "Women in Social Reform Movements." In

*The Nineteenth Century.* Vol. 1, *Women and Religion in America.* Edited by Rosemary Radford Ruether and Rosemary Skinner Keller. San Francisco: Harper and Row, 1981.

Gilkes, Cheryl Townsend. "The Role of Women in the Sanctified Church." *Journal of Religious Thought* 43 (spring-summer 1986).

Gordon, Ann D., and Mari Jo Buhle. "Sex and Class in Colonial and Nineteenth-Century America," *Liberating Women's History: Theoretical and Critical Essays.* Chicago: University of Illinois Press, 1976.

Grant, Jacquelyn. "Womanist Theology: Black Women's Experience as a Source for Doing Theology, with Special Reference to Christology." *Journal of the Interdenominational Theological Center* 13 (spring 1986): 195–212.

Hamilton, Tullia K. Brown. "The National Association of Colored Women, 1986 to 1920." Ph.D. diss., Emory University, 1978.

Harley, Sharon. "Anna J. Cooper: A Voice for Black Women," *The Afro-American Woman: Struggles and Images,* edited by Sharon Harley and Rosalyn Terborg-Penn. Port Washington, N.Y.: Kennikat Press, 1978.

———. "Mary Church Terrell: Genteel Militant," *Black Leaders of the Nineteenth Century,* edited by Leon Litwack and August Meier. Urbana: University of Illinois Press, 1988.

———. "Northern Black Female Workers: Jacksonian Era," *The Afro-American Woman: Struggles and Images,* edited by Sharon Harley and Rosalyn Terborg-Penn. Port Washington, N.Y.: Kennikat Press, 1978.

———. "Black Women in a Southern City: Washington, D.C., 1890–1920," *Sex, Race, and the Role of Women in the South,* edited by Joan V. Hawks and Sheila L. Skemp. Jackson: University of Mississippi Press, 1983.

Harper, Frances. "Coloured Women of America." *Englishman's Review* 15 (1878): 10–15.

———. "National Women's Christian Temperance Union." *A.M.E. Church Review* 5 (1889): 242–45.

———. "The Women's Christian Temperance Union and the Colored Woman." *A.M.E. Church Review.* 4 (1888): 314.

Harrison, Beverly. "The Early Feminists and the Clergy: A Case Study in Dynamics of Secularization." *Making the Connections,* edited by Carol S. Robb. Boston: Beacon Press, 1985.

Higginbotham, Evelyn Brooks. *Righteous Discontent: The Women's Movement in the Black Baptist Church, 1880–1920.* Cambridge, Mass.: Harvard University Press, 1993.

Hill, Ruth. "Lifting As We Climb: Black Women's Organizations, 1890–1935." *Radcliffe Quarterly* 70 (March 1984): 24–26.

*A History of the Club Movement Among the Colored Women of the United*

*States of America*. Washington, D.C.: National Association of Colored Women's Clubs, Inc., 1902.

Hobson, E. C., and C. E. Hopkins. *Report Concerning the Colored Women of the South*. Baltimore: Slater Fund, 1896.

Holt, Thomas C. *Black Over White: Negro Political Leadership in South Carolina During Reconstruction*. Urbana: University of Illinois Press, 1977.

————. "The Lonely Warrior: Ida B. Wells-Barnett and the Struggle for Black Leadership," *Black Leaders of the Twentieth Century*, edited by John Hope Franklin and August Meier. Urbana: University of Illinois Press, 1982.

Hooks, Bell. *Ain't I a Woman: Black Women and Feminism*. Boston: South End Press, 1981.

————. *Feminist Theory: From Margin to Center*. Boston: South End Press, 1984.

Horton, H. O. "Freedom's Yoke: Gender Conventions Among Antebellum Free Blacks." *Feminist Studies* 12 (spring 1986): 51–76.

Hull, Gloria T., Patricia Bell Scott, and Barbara Smith, eds. *All the Women Are White, All the Blacks Are Men, but Some of Us Are Brave*. New York: Feminist Press, 1982.

Hundley, Mary S. "The National Association of Colored Women." *Opportunity: Journal of Negro Life*, June 1925, 185.

Hunton, Addie W. "The Detroit Convention of the National Association of Colored Women." *Voice of the Negro* 3 (August 1906): 589–93.

————. "The National Association of Colored Women: Its Real Significance." *Colored American* 14 (July 1908).

Jones, Anna H. "The American Colored Woman." *Voice of the Negro* 2 (October 1905): 692–94.

————. "A Century's Progress of the American Colored Woman." *Voice of the Negro* 2 (September 1905): 631–33.

Jones, Jacqueline. *Labor of Love, Labor of Sorrow*. New York: Basic Books, 1985.

Jordan, June. "Where Is the Love?" *Women's Consciousness, Women's Conscience*. New York: Winston Press, 1985.

Lerner, Gerda. "Early Community Work of Black Club Women." *Journal of Negro History* 59 (1974).

————. *The Majority Finds Its Past: Placing Women in America History*. New York: Oxford University Press, 1979.

————. "Placing Women in History: A 1975 Perspective" and "New Approaches to the Study of Women in American History," *Liberating Women's History: Theoretical and Critical Essays*. Chicago: University of Illinois Press, 1976.

Lerner, Gerda, ed. *Black Women in White America: A Documentary History*. New York: Vintage Books, 1973.

Litwack, Leon F. *Been in the Storm So Long: The Aftermath of Slavery.* New York: Knopf, 1979.

Lynch, Mary. "Social Status and Needs of the Colored Woman," *The United Negro,* edited by J. W. E. Bowen. Atlanta: D. E. Luther, 1902.

Majors, Monroe A. *Noted Negro Women: Their Triumphs and Activities.* Freeport, N.Y.: Books for Libraries Press, 1971, reprinted, 1983.

Meltzer, Milton. *In Their Own Words: A History of the American Negro 1865–1916.* New York: Crowell, 1965.

Moses, Wilson Jeremiah. *The Golden Age of Black Nationalism, 1850–1925.* New York: Oxford University Press, 1978.

Mossell, Gertrude S. *The Work of the Afro-American Woman.* Philadelphia: George S. Ferguson, 1894; reprinted, New York: Books for Libraries Press, 1971.

Murray, Anna E. "The Negro Woman." *Southern Workman* 33 (April 1904): 232–34.

"National Association of Colored Women's Clubs." *Southern Workman,* December 1922, 543–45.

Neverdon-Morton, Cynthia. "The Black Woman's Struggle for Equality in the South, 1895–1925," *The Afro-American Woman: Struggles and Images,* edited by Sharon Harley and Rosalyn Terborg-Penn. Port Washington, N.Y.: Kennikat Press, 1978.

———. *Afro-American Women of the South and the Advancement of the Race, 1895–1925.* Knoxville: University of Tennessee Press, 1989.

Papachristou, Judith. "Associationism and Reform: 1890–1920; Black Women's Organizations," *Women Together.* New York: Knopf, 1976.

Porter, Dorothy. *Early Negro Writing: 1760–1837.* Boston: Beacon Press, 1971.

———. "Organized Activities of Negro Literary Societies, 1828–1846." *Journal of Negro Education* 5 (October 1936): 555–76.

Richardson, Marilyn. "Three Women in the Black Church: An Introduction," *Black Women and Religion: A Bibliography.* Boston: G. K. Hall, 1980.

Richardson, Marilyn, ed. *Maria W. Stewart: America's First Black Woman Political Writer.* Bloomington: Indiana University Press, 1987.

Rodgers-Rose, LaFrances, ed. *The Black Woman.* Beverly Hills: Sage, 1980.

Rothman, Shelia M. *Women's Proper Place: A History of Changing Ideals and Practices, 1870 to the Present.* New York: Basic Books, 1978.

Robinson, Wilhelmina. *Historical Negro Biographies: International Library of Negro Life and History.* New York: Publishers Co., 1967.

Ryan, Mary. "The Power of Women's Networks: A Case Study of Female Moral Reform in Antebellum America." *Feminist Studies* 5 (spring 1979).

Scruggs, Lawson. *Women of Distinction: Remarkable in Works and Invincible in Character.* Raleigh, N.C.: L. A. Scruggs, 1893.

Shepperd, Gladys Byrum. *Mary Church Terrell: Respectable Person.* Baltimore: Human Relations Press, 1959.

Shockley, Ann Allen. "The Negro Woman in Retrospect." *Negro History Bulletin* 29 (December 1963): 55–56, 62, 70.

Silone-Yates, Josephine. "The National Association of Colored Women." *Voice of the Negro* 1 (July 1904): 238.

———. "Women's World." *Colored American,* 8 May 1902, 2.

Sochen, June. *Herstory: A Woman's View of American History.* New York: Alfred Publishing, 1974.

Sterling, Dorothy. *Black Foremothers, Three Lives.* New York: Feminist Press, 1979.

———. *We Are Your Sisters: Black Women in the Nineteenth Century.* New York: W. W. Norton, 1984.

Stewart, Maria W. *Productions of Mrs. Maria W. Stewart.* Boston: W. Lloyd Garrison and Knapp, 1832.

Terborg-Penn, Rosalyn. "Afro-Americans in the Struggle for Woman Suffrage." Ph.D. diss., Howard University, 1977.

———. "Black Male Perspectives on the Nineteenth Century Woman," *The Afro-American Woman: Struggles and Images,* edited by Sharon Harley and Rosalyn Terborg-Penn. Port Washington, N.Y.: Kennikat Press, 1978.

———. "Discrimination Against Afro-American Women in the Women's Movement," *The Afro-American Woman: Struggles and Images,* edited by Sharon Harley and Rosalyn Terborg-Penn. Port Washington, N.Y.: Kennikat Press, 1978.

Terrell, Mary Church. *A Colored Woman in a White World.* Washington, D.C.: Randell, 1940.

———. "The International Congress of Women." *Voice of the Negro* 1 (December 1904): 454–61.

———. "Lynching from a Negro's Point of View." *North American Review* 178 (July 1904): 853–98.

———. Mary Church Terrell Papers. Library of Congress. Washington, D.C.

———. "The Progress of Colored Women." *Voice of the Negro* 1 (July 1904): 291–94.

Thompson, Mildred. "Ida B. Wells-Barnett: An Exploratory Study of an American Black Woman, 1893–1930." Ph.D. diss., George Washington University, 1979.

Townes, Emilie M. *Womanist Justice, Womanist Hope.* Atlanta: Scholars Press, 1993.

Tucker, David M. "Miss Ida B. Wells and the Memphis Lynching." *Phylon* 32 (summer 1971): 112–22.

Ware, Cellestine. "Problems of 19th Century Feminism," *Beyond Liberalism: The New Left Views American History*, edited by Irwin Unger. Waltham, Mass.: Xerox College Publishing, 1971.

Washington, Mrs. Booker T. "Social Improvement of the Plantation Woman." *Voice of the Negro* 1 (July 1904): 288–90.

Washington, Margaret. "Club Work Among Negro Women," *Progress of a Race*, edited by J. Nichols and W. Crogman. Naperville, Ill.: J. L. Nichols, 1929.

Watkins, Frances Ellen. "Our Great Want." *Anglo-African Magazine* 1 (1859): 160.

Webb, Lillian Ashcroft. "Black Women and Religion in the Colonial Period." In *The Colonial and Revolutionary Periods*. Vol. 2, *Women and Religion in America*. Edited by Rosemary Radford Ruether and Rosemary Skinner Keller. San Francisco: Harper and Row, 1983.

Wells-Barnett, Ida. The Ida B. Wells Papers. Special Collections. Joseph Regenstein Library, University of Chicago, Chicago, Illinois.

———. *On Lynchings*. New York: Ano Press, 1969.

———. *A Red Record, Tabulated Statistics and Alleged Causes of Lynchings in the U.S., 1892–1893–1894*. New York: Arno Press, 1969. (Reprint of 1895 edition)

———. *Southern Horrors: Lynch Law in All Its Phases*. New York: Arno Press, 1969. (Reprint of 1892 edition)

Wesley, Charles H. *The History of the National Association of Colored Women's Clubs: A Legacy of Service*. Washington, D.C.: National Association of Colored Women's Clubs, 1984.

White, Deborah Gray. *Ain't I a Woman: Female Slaves in the Antebellum South*. New York: W. W. Norton, 1985.

Williams, Delores. "Womanist Theology: Black Women's Voices." *Christianity and Crisis*, 2 March 1987, 66–70.

Williams, Emily H. "The Club Movement Among the Colored Women." *Voice of the Negro* 1 (1904): 101.

———. "The National Association of Colored Women." *Southern Workman* 43 (December 1914): 564–66.

Williams, Fannie Barrier. "The Club Movement Among Colored Women of America," *A New Negro for a New Century*. New York: Arno Press, 1969. (Reprint of 1900 edition)

———. "Club Movement Among Negro Women," *Progress of a Race*, edited by J. Nichols and W. Crogman. Atlanta: J. L. Nichols, 1903.

———. "The Colored Girl." *Voice of the Negro* 2 (June 1905): 400–403.

———. "The Colored Woman and Her Part in Race Regeneration," *A New Negro for a New Century*. New York: Arno Press, 1969. (Reprint of 1900 edition)

———. "The Negro and Public Opinion." *Voice of the Negro* 1 (January 1904): 31–32.

———. *The Present Status and Intellectual Progress of Colored Women*. Chicago, 1893.

Williams, Sylvanie. "The Social Status of the Negro Woman." *Voice of the Negro* 1 (July 1904): 298–300.

# Index

convention movement, 28;
depression, 1; development,
43; elite, 4, 10, 17, 25, 35, 38, 40,
43, 66; experience, 17; false
consciousness, 19; family, 75;
farmers, 42; free, 23–31, 35, 40,
48, 50; labor, 32–33, 37, 73;
leaders, 18, 29, 35; leadership,
36; liberals, 19, 88; liberation,
1, 4–8, 10–12, 14, 18–20, 75–77,
82, 85, 87, 90–91, 93; life, 59;
lower class, 17, 23–24, 38, 89;
majority, 3; married women,
53; masses, 4, 17, 88; men, 3,
67, 77; middle class, 4, 15–19,
23–24, 28, 87–89; migration of
women, 53; mulatto, 23, 25, 35,
40; nationalism, 28, 44;
oppression, 1–3, 16, 18–19,
55–57, 61, 70, 78, 81, 84, 93;
poor, 17, 30; professional, 79;
professional women, 52;
"rapist" myth, 52; self-
understanding, 44; single
women, 53; sociology, 7;
southern urban, 38;
stratification, 21, 31–32, 34,
36–37, 40, 42, 54, 87;
subculture, 87; teachers, 50;
underclass, 13–16, 18; in
United States, 10; upper class,
17, 19, 23, 24, 89; urban, 38;
washerwomen, 49, 51;
womanhood, 49–50, 52, 54, 79;
womanist theology, 2; women,
2–5, 45, 47–49, 51–52, 54, 57,
61, 63, 67–68, 70, 74–75, 77,
79–80, 93–95; women's club
movement, 1, 6, 47, 61, 65–67,
71, 75, 77, 79, 90, 95; working
class, 51
Blackwell, James, 9
Boycotting, as measure by
women's club movement, 73

Burroughs, Nannie Helen, 60–61,
72
Business: banking, 40; real estate,
40

Capitalism, 2, 3, 8, 12, 16;
democracy, 8; exploitation,
15–16; northern industrial, 33;
system, 44
Caste-class oppression, 43
Caste-class structure, 29, 32, 34
Charleston, black landholdings
in, 24
Chicago: black elite in, 40; *Daily
News*, 74; NACW convention
in, 74
Children, 64, 67–68, 74–75;
welfare, 81
Christ, 95, 100; as liberator, 86; as
redeemer, 94
Christian ethical process, 100
Christian love, 99
Christian morality, 94, 99
Christian moral vision, 97, 99
Church(es), 38, 54, 60, 63, 78,
94–97; African, 31; Baptist, 40;
membership, 40; Methodist,
40; work, 63
Civil rights, 14–16, 43, 87
Class, 6, 8, 13–16, 21, 25, 48, 89,
94; consciousness, 11
Classism, 66, 84
Cleveland, Ohio, black elite in,
40
Clinton, Catherine, 50
Club(s), 4, 62; black club
movement leaders, 66; Black
National Women's Movement,
1, 6, 47, 61–63, 66, 77, 80–81,
93; church-affiliated, 78; ethic,
84, 86, 88; professional, 62;
movement, 20, 47, 54, 62, 82;
social, 38, 77–78; southern, 75;
and women, 68, 80–81, 83, 85,